Advance Praise for *Shipshape*

"As the former State Auditor for Kentucky, I witnessed dozens of nonprofit organizations whose governance was lacking because their boards and staff were often unprepared and inadequately trained. This clear and compelling publication by Eric Schmall offers a valuable roadmap to put any nonprofit on the path to successful management. His inspired use of clever metaphors serves to actively engage the reader in learning from the helpful tools he provides."

-Crit Luallen, former State Auditor
Commonwealth of Kentucky

"This is easy reading but with powerful concepts. Because we learn best from metaphors and stories, the impact of this book will be long-term. Best of all, it is enjoyable to be introduced to or reminded of what our responsibilities are as nonprofit board members. After reading it, my perspectives were reinforced and, more important, I reflected on my contributions to the nonprofits I've served as a board member. A great resource!"

-Robert L. Taylor, Dean Emeritus
University of Louisville School of Business

"Whether your nonprofit organization is new or well seasoned, it makes no difference. *Shipshape* is the perfect read and field guide to get everyone on board. In three short sessions, Eric Schmall helped right our ship that was listing after an unplanned, tumultuous leadership change in the face of 63 years of measurable success. We owe Eric a debt of gratitude."

- Barbara Sexton Smith, President & CEO
Fund for the Arts

"*Shipshape* lays out in clear terms the issues related to nonprofit governance and, through effective use of metaphor, engages the reader in deep learning."

-Deborah Walker, President & CEO
Collaborative for Teaching and Learning

"I wish Ms. Mildred Horn were here today to congratulate Eric on writing this very helpful book to bring clarity to the critical work of nonprofit governance and stewardship."

-H. Scott Davis Jr., Manager,
Mildred V. Horn Foundation

"I am so proud to have served and currently serve as a Trustee/Director of many nonprofit boards. But...I surely wish I had this book years ago...How much richer would those boards be today. Great information—thanks for making it clear and presenting it in a fashion that we can all understand, comprehend, and implement. All boards should adopt Shipshape...the value added is immediate."

-Marita Willis, Vice President, Community Consultant
Community Develpment Banking
PNC Bank

"Eric Schmall succeeds beautifully in demystifying nonprofit agency governance, leadership, and purpose through a clear and powerful use of metaphor. The work reminds me of one of Seth Godin's blogs entitled "All Boats Leak," wherein Godin stated that "there's always a defect, always a slow drip, somewhere. Every plan, every organization, every venture has a glitch. The question isn't, "Is this perfect?" The question is, "Will this get me there?" Shipshape makes it easier for all of us to maintain our focus on what really matters. It's a very valuable read."

- Joe Tolan, President & CEO
Metro United Way

"Have you ever been in one of those meetings that starts off well with a shared desire to establish a collective vision and create an impactful strategy that will advance the mission, but then all too quickly the productivity of the meeting is derailed? Instead of achieving agreement on action items, you spend the first half of the meeting debating the semantics.

"If you want to give your board members a head start in this conversation, Shipshape is a great accelerant. This book provides everyone a shared understanding of the terms and concepts that are most important in moving an organization forward. The use of the ship metaphor throughout the book helps make all the concepts stick with the reader. So when it's time to actually start the planning you can move right to action, wasting no time agreeing on what the definition of 'is' is!"

-Cynthia Spalding Knapek, President
Leadership Louisville Center

"Having worked with nonprofit agencies for over twenty years, I have seen a variety of approaches to strategic planning from the complicated to the complex. However, by taking a holistic view of an organization's strategic planning process and its many moving parts, Eric Schmall has made it manageable, with simplicity and clarity. The clever nautical metaphor is imaginative and practical."

-Mason B. Rummel, President
J. Graham Brown Foundation, Inc.

You can't cross the sea merely by standing and staring at the water.

-Rabindranath Tagore

ShipShape

An Uncomplicated Guide to Navigating your Nonprofit

Eric Schmall

Center for Nonprofit Excellence
Louisville, Kentucky

CENTER FOR
**NONPROFIT
EXCELLENCE**
Your Excellence is Our Passion

Illustrations by
Chris Austerman, student intern
Kentucky School of Art

Shipshape: An Uncomplicated Guide to Navigating Your Nonprofit
Legal Copy Page (03.18.13)
Copyright © 2013 by Center for Nonprofit Excellence

Published by Old Stone Press
an imprint of J. H. Clark & Associates, Inc.
Louisville, Kentucky 40207 USA
www.OldStonePress.com

CONTRIBUTORS

Book Design & Illustrations by Chris Austerman, student intern
Kentucky School of Art in Louisville, Kentucky
with special thanks to Annie Langan, Professor of Photography + Multimedia
www.KentuckySchoolofArt.org

Lori Brown Patrick, Grammarwitch, LLC

Elizabeth Perry Spalding, 21 Skye Design

First Edition: April 2013
Printed in the United States of America
Shipshape by Eric Schmall
ISBN: 978-1-938462-06-1
Library of Congress Cataloging-in-Publication Data
Has been filed for:

DEDICATION

FOR ALL NONPROFIT "SHIPS" & THOSE WHO SAIL THEM.

Acknowledgements

The ideas in this book have evolved from my consulting experience with hundreds of nonprofits over the past twelve years regarding board governance, strategic planning, management, leadership, and best practices. I am grateful for the benefit of working with each of them. With every group I worked with, I learned something new, added to my experience and, by that, I trust, improved my ability to help each of the succeeding groups with whom I was privileged to work.

I wish to express my thanks to the Center for Nonprofit Excellence's board of directors for their authorization to pursue publishing these concepts. I am especially grateful for the encouragement and freedom to develop this model of governance given to me by the Center's CEO, Kevin Connelly, under whose able command it has been my honor to serve during these past twelve years.

I owe equal thanks to the Harrison County Community Foundation, the Cralle Foundation, and another local foundation that has requested anonymity, all of whom have been steadfast supporters of the Center and have generously contributed to this book's development through their financial support.

Finally, and in greatest measure, I express my thanks to my wife, Barbara, for her indefatigable moral support, patience, and confidence in me as I brought these ideas together in this work.

AUTHOR'S NOTE

The descriptive stories used to illustrate the primary point for each chapter contain only fictitious names of organizations and individuals. As an integral part of consulting with organizations, I adhere to the precept of confidentiality to preserve the privacy of all. While I have witnessed the examples of behaviors, both exemplary and dysfunctional, in these anecdotes, the circumstances, characters, and organizations portrayed in these stories are composites, altered and blended in the specifics, in order to represent the concept I am attempting to illustrate without violating the fundamental principle of confidentiality. Any resemblance of such a composite organization or individual to any actual nonprofit or person is purely coincidental.

TABLE OF CONTENTS

Chapter 1: Unleash the Power of a Metaphor!   **Page 1**

Metaphors are figurative ways of describing things. We use them all the time to better understand and communicate. For example, "life is a highway" evokes a picture of life being a journey along a well-established road. Metaphors can be useful in clarifying how nonprofits should ideally operate.

Chapter 2: Choosing the Ideal Metaphor: Ship of State   **Page 9**

People use all sorts of metaphors to describe organizations. Some think of their organization as a family. Others may think of their business as a machine, or something organic, like a living plant. Among the easiest and most adaptive for our purposes, I propose another popular and easily understood metaphor: the organization as a ship.

Chapter 3: The Ultimate Destination: Vision and Values   **Page 19**

Ships are built to travel to specific destinations. For a nonprofit ship, this destination represents its vision—the ideal future shore where this ship promises to deliver its travelers.

Chapter 4: The Shipbuilder(s): The Founder(s)   **Page 33**

Nonprofits begin with a dream. Those who dream about a better future—the community that is somehow improved—are the ones who act as the prime movers, the ones who decide that a vessel must be constructed in order to undertake the journey.

While the vision represents the ultimate destination, the mission describes the actions the ship takes to move purposely in that direction. The ship moves toward its ultimate destination when it is powered by the sails, winds, and currents comprised of successful programs.

A nonprofit's vision may be focused on helping certain individuals, or a whole community, or the entire world. No matter the scale, those served represent the passengers on this ship that is bound to deliver them to the ideal, envisioned shore.

The group that has the highest responsibility for the ship's safe and successful passage can be found in the board of directors. They collectively act, through their supervision and strategic foresight, as guarantors to the passengers that the ship will deliver them to the destination.

The people who actually operate the ship, the ones who translate the owners' strategic directions into tactical, executable activities, are the staff and volunteers, led by the able command of the captain.

Seafaring has enough challenges without having to contend with the potential confusion—if not outright chaos—that will result if the owners, captain, crew, and passengers don't understand and respect their roles and proper responsibilities.

Chapter 15: Convoys, Fleets, and Flotillas: Joining with Others   **Page 207**

The vast challenges of the sea journey can be confronted and overcome through joining with other vessels that will help share the risks, pool resources, and expand the range of talent, knowledge, and leadership.

Chapter 16: Homeward Bound   **Page 223**

The ship may be on a journey that will require generations of leadership, endless refitting of the ship's timbers, and countless sequential owners. Despite those changes, to paraphrase Senator Ted Kennedy, the ship goes on, the cause endures, the hope still lives, and the dream shall never die.

Nice! ☺

FOREWORD

The modern-day nonprofit sector is allowed considerable freedom to govern itself, so long as it operates in a manner consistent with its sanctioned and stated benefits to society.

No one owns the nonprofit, save the societal guardians known as the board of directors.

When the board, along with staff leadership, work well together, some part of our community becomes perceptibly better.

When it does not, headlines may scream of its ineffectiveness, dereliction of duty, unethical behavior, and even criminal misconduct. Or—more quietly, perhaps, but just as tragically—opportunities for a better world are squandered.

Much has been written about the complex nature of how a board can effectively frame and support the work of a nonprofit organization. Still, confusion abounds.

Eric Schmall began to help nonprofit boards work better—and nonprofit organizations to plan more strategically—twelve years ago when he allied his civic quest and his employment with the Center for Nonprofit Excellence (CNPE).

Eric's role in helping to advance CNPE's mission was initially aided by lessons he had learned during his distinguished leadership service in the US Air Force, a successful career in the corporate sector, and leading and facilitating groups of people during periods of organizational change.

He possesses, as you will witness from the engaging pages that follow, the ability to offer examples that bring real clarity to the purpose and role of the board – especially in the context of its relationship to the staff and the CEO.

Now equipped with hundreds of board planning sessions and retreats, Eric offers us an uncomplicated guide that clarifies the board's role by illuminating its deeper purpose. Like any human life or organizational entity, when true purpose is wed to its companion role, dynamic power is simultaneously unleashed and harnessed for the greater good.

Affirmed by hundreds of notes and feedback comments on Eric's work through the Center for Nonprofit Excellence, his exceptional abilities have aided scores of boards in their quest to better govern, lead, and support. Now, *Shipshape: An Uncomplicated Guide to Navigating Your Nonprofit* consolidates many of his insights and stories into a practical guide for board work. It is a must-read for anyone who seriously undertakes the noble service of board leadership.

Kevin J. Connelly
Executive Director, Center for Nonprofit Excellence

PREFACE

"The only difference between us and the *Titanic* is that the *Titanic* had a band," one frustrated board member whispered to me during a break at a board planning retreat. I had to agree, their nonprofit "ship" was listing badly in the water. That clever observation reminded me how organizations can be thought of as ships and, more ominously, how closely some organizational ships might resemble that tragic ocean liner.

At the next retreat I led, I decided to use this ship metaphor to see if it wouldn't help engage the board's participation more successfully. I drew a ship's outline on a whiteboard and asked the retreat participants, "If your nonprofit were a ship, how would you describe it?" That quick nautical illustration sparked a sudden attention-grabbing moment, dispelling the typical Saturday morning retreat lethargy. Several people started offering ideas.

"There's a hole in the hull and we're taking on water," one cried out.

"That's because of the rough seas we're in," exclaimed another.

"No, it's because we never take time to maintain the ship," offered a third. As I jotted down these ideas and drew squiggly symbolic pictures all around my elementary, symbolic ship to represent these characteristics, the room became more energized. Staying true to our model of the organization as a ship, the group launched itself into one of the most productive and creative planning retreats I had ever witnessed.

Over time, I continued to employ this metaphor in different retreat settings, sometimes as a way to educate boards on their role, sometimes to help boards and staff personnel think about their individual roles and the proper boundaries of their responsibilities. After I had begun trying out this approach, I was fortunate to be able to take a series of short vacations during which I found myself as a passenger on a number of waterborne vessels.

These ranged from a two-person kayak in the Pacific Northwest, to a modest riverboat floating down the Nile, to a family houseboat at a state park lake, and finally to a majestic, five thousand-passenger cruise ship plying its way through the Caribbean. In every instance, I was literally experiencing the metaphor, watching the interaction of the ship, the seas, the weather, the crew, the passengers, the detours, and the steady advance toward the destination. Every time I returned to work from one of these trips, the reinforced power of the metaphor seemed increasingly easy for me to suggest and use in each board retreat or board education event—a simple way to clarify the abstract concepts that make up nonprofit governance, management, and operations.

The unfailing success of this method led me to write this book. I want to demystify—for board members, staff, volunteers, or anyone else who wants to more thoroughly understand how nonprofits can function well—a means of clearly thinking and communicating about issues such as governance, management, leadership, and purpose. I want it to illuminate how to think about the boundaries between nonprofit boards and staff functions, how to understand the value of vision, the critical need for strategic planning, and the fundamental best practices that lead to mission success.

Even more significant, this work is intended to be a guide for those who are considering joining a nonprofit board, so they can more easily and quickly understand how nonprofits function and how enticing, rewarding, and critically important their role will be in governing the organization.

Plenty of books have been written about nonprofit governance and management. But this one is different. This one is designed to be the clearest and most engaging means of understanding and applying the best principles of responsible governance and management. This book is far from academic, though it is based upon solid academic research and field experience. It's meant to be easily read, easily understood, and easily applied—a truly useable workbook for nonprofit organizations that want to improve their process of understanding how to govern, manage, and succeed.

INTRODUCTION

If you're one of the millions of people in this nation involved in helping a nonprofit organization succeed—as a board member, an executive director, a staff member, or a volunteer—and you're perplexed over the nonprofit structure, organization, or how things *ought* to be, then this book was written to give you the answers you seek.

It's meant to offer a simple, quickly understandable way to illustrate how to think about big issues that frustrate a lot of well-intentioned participants. For example, the difference and relationship between a nonprofit's vision and mission, the roles and proper boundaries between board, staff, volunteers, and donors, the reasons for and differences between good governance and good management—all of these are critical issues to get right.

But it's been hard to find simple explanations—until now.

In the seemingly endless tempest of the Great Recession, there's never been a more urgent need for competent leadership, governance, and management to help nonprofit organizations sustain themselves. In spite of that need, well-intentioned board members and staff executives struggle to find the clarity necessary to identify the key ideas that will ensure success.

This workbook proposes to be a substantial help in finding that clarity. Its purpose is to shine a light upon the pathway so that nonprofit boards and staff can discover a renewed clarity about the fundamentals, and assure mission success.

In my last twelve years of working with hundreds of nonprofit boards in leading strategic planning retreats, one thing has become abundantly clear: people simply lack an agreed-upon, comprehensible, working language to deal with such abstract ideas as governance, leadership, and management issues. Board members struggle with the differences between vision and mission. They confuse the boundaries between board and staff roles.

Few appreciate the advantages of or the methods used to formulate strategic planning.

In my consulting practice, I have discovered a promising way to resolve this major problem. By using the power of a metaphor, a model way of thinking that takes these abstract terms and gives them a concrete representation, the confusion evaporates, productive conversations finally appear, and solid, useful solutions and plans emerge.

By using this metaphorical model over the past year, I have repeatedly witnessed participants recognizing with deeper clarity the problems they are encountering. This illuminating approach enables them to move toward better problem recognition and resolution. I have repeatedly heard board members make claims that for the first time they finally understand their roles, or that they can now truly grasp the real value they bring in their governance responsibilities. Armed with that greater understanding, they then move more confidently toward building better strategies and making more informed decisions.

This consequential breakthrough in thinking, discussing, and forging effective plans needs to be shared with wider circles than I can reach through my limited ability to personally engage with nonprofit organizations. In order to share these concepts to the broadest possible good effect, I have resolved to construct this workbook. It is a means to invite any nonprofit group to apply this simple yet powerful formula of taking the following complex issues and translating them into easily understood metaphorical models of simple but compelling rules, roles, and activities:

- The Ultimate Destination: The vision, the promised arrival port for those whom the organization serves
- Shipbuilder: The founder(s), the person(s) who possessed the original vision and took action to create the organization
- Propelling the ship: The mission and programs that move the ship toward the ultimate destination.

- Passengers: Those who are served by the mission, who are on the ship being taken to the promised destination
- Ship's owners: The board of directors who represent the passengers and guarantee that the ship's functions, progress, and capacity will get the passengers to the promised port
- Captain and crew: The executive director and staff (including volunteers) who have the responsibilities of sailing the ship and caring for the passengers
- Boundaries: Proper relationships between the executive director, crew, owners, and passengers
- Charting the course: Setting the strategic direction of the ship based on the passengers' needs, the capabilities of the ship, and the external environment filled with favorable (winds that fill the sails) and unfavorable influences (storms, reefs) that affect the ship's journey
- Investors: Those who believe in the ship's destiny and help by sending their contributions and resources to ensure that the ship can remain seaworthy and journey forward
- Lifeboats and life preservers: Identifying and dealing with risks to ensure the journey's success
- Beacons and signals: Ways to communicate with passengers, investors, and the public
- Lighthouse, buoys, harbor lights, and sea lore: The guiding standards that keep the ship from crashing on the reefs or rocks of malfeasance, mismanagement, or poor governance
- Convoys, fleets, and flotillas: Gathering with the other ships that sail on the grand seas—many of whom are on similar journeys, carry similar passengers, and face similar challenges—toward a common purpose through cooperation, coordination and collaboration.

linkages

This is written in a workbook format. In each chapter, I begin with an essay describing a key aspect of nonprofit success. I summarize each chapter with the key points to apply. I offer a short list of questions to stimulate the conversation and the construction of your newly clarified view of your organization, based on the chapter's ideas. At the conclusion of each chapter, I offer a fictional narrative of a nonprofit group engaged in dealing with some subject based on that chapter's theme. Those narratives can be used for further discussion if you're using this workbook as a team. Some of these stories have happy resolutions. Others end more messily. All are helpful, given this wisdom: If you can't be an example, be a warning.

Each chapter is self-contained. Readers can feel free to dip into any chapter to delve into the area they feel is most important to them. If the fictional narrative section at the end of each chapter doesn't seem to add interest, I suggest skipping it. It is there because, in my experience, the power of storytelling, combined with developing this method, has made the learning exponentially more powerful.

CHAPTER 1

UNLEASH THE POWER OF A METAPHOR!

The soul cannot think without a picture.
—Aristotle

L et's begin with a brief definition. The word *metaphor* comes from the Greek term meaning "transfer" or "carry over." People use metaphors as a means of both understanding and experiencing an unfamiliar thing in terms of another, more familiar subject. Isaac Newton used metaphors to explain how the heavens moved by describing them as giant mechanisms, similar to machines like clocks, familiar to his readers in the eighteenth century. Einstein thought in metaphorical terms as he mused over aspects of his relativity theory, imagining himself riding on a beam of light to contemplate his hypotheses about time and space. These sorts of thinking "pictures" reduce the otherwise daunting challenge of understanding very abstract theories by translating them into much more understandable ideas.

Authors Michael Berman and David Brown, in their work The Power of Metaphor, suggest that "if a picture is worth a thousand words, then a metaphor is worth a thousand pictures."

Metaphors are found everywhere. Most of the time people don't realize how frequently they witness others using metaphors in their everyday lives. Research cited in James Geary's book *I Is an Other* suggests that we "utter one metaphor for every ten to twenty-five words or use about six metaphors a minute."[1]

Literature brims with metaphors, conveying meaning and deepening our understanding. Shakespeare's famous metaphor in his play *As You Like It*— "All the world's a stage/And all the men and women merely players"— still resonates four hundred years later. In that memorable passage, Shakespeare describes people's lives as if they were actors playing roles through their brief appearances on life's "stage."

---

[1] Geary, *I Is an Other*, 5.

It is well accepted that "a picture is worth a thousand words." Pictures allow us to literally "see" or understand things much more quickly, with a clarity that words might never achieve. Authors Michael Berman and David Brown, in their work *The Power of Metaphor*, suggest that "if a picture is worth a thousand words, then a metaphor is worth a thousand pictures."[2]

Metaphors help us clarify complex ideas, understand interconnections, evoke powerful emotions, and communicate persuasively. Think of how political leaders inspire vision and arouse energy by offering the public metaphorical images. For example, in his 1961 inaugural address, President John F. Kennedy exhorted his contemporaries to face the challenges confronting the United States when he said, "the torch has been passed to a new generation—born in this century." Obviously no actual torch passes between generations, but the phrase certainly demonstrates a clear picture of a retiring group entrusting leadership, responsibility, and traditions to younger people. The metaphor was particularly poignant since Kennedy, then 43, was assuming the presidency from the outgoing President Eisenhower, age 71.

---

[2] Berman and Brown, *The Power of Metaphor*, 4.

Organizational Metaphors

Business theorists have used metaphors as a means to help us understand how organizations function. Gareth Morgan, in his incisive work, *Images of Organization*[3], offers nine different metaphorical ways of thinking about corporations. Among the more popular metaphors are those which describe organizations as machines, living organisms, or political systems. In any of these instances, the different metaphors propose a framework describing how the organization performs, what's working well or what is not, and how to move forward. The metaphor that an individual selects to help understand and explain organizational behavior makes a huge difference in that organization's character. If a chief executive officer thinks about the organization as a mechanical device, then all the components—even the employees—could be thought of as interchangeable cogs. While that's easy to envision, one might wonder how such a metaphor might color the CEO's behavior in managing those human "cogs."

Application to Nonprofit Organizations

Nonprofit organizations are equally filled with all types of abstract concepts and functions such as board governance, the role of leadership, the function of management, resource development, the idea of "capacity building," best practices, and interrelationships of responsibility between

---

[3] Morgan, *Images of Organization*.

staff, executive directors, board members, volunteers, and donors. People who work to make a nonprofit succeed all yearn for a clear, logical, easily explained understanding of how all these abstractions are supposed to work in harmony. In other words, they seek a functioning metaphor.

To fulfill this need, we need to construct an extended metaphor, one that can successfully tie together all the abstractions in nonprofit organizations, using one coherent theme. The next chapter begins the process.

Compass Points

-◇- Metaphors are a natural and common way in which we communicate with one another.

-◇- Metaphors are a key means by which we can take abstract ideas and convert them into easily understood and convincing ideas.

-◇- The purposeful use of the right metaphor can open whole new vistas of understanding in leading and helping nonprofits succeed.

Points to Consider

1. Listen to the way people you talk to use metaphors to describe their world. Reflect on how the metaphors they used helped you understand and react.

_____

_____

_____

_____

_____

_____

_____

2. Pay attention to the metaphors you use to describe your world. What are your favorites? Why do you choose them?

_____

_____

_____

_____

_____

_____

_____

3. Watch how journalists, reporters, and commentators use metaphors to deliver news and opinions. Does their choice of specific metaphors influence you in any way?

_____

_____

_____

_____

_____

_____

_____

4. What metaphors have you seen used to describe your nonprofit? Which one seems to work the best in offering clarity and understanding?

_____

_____

_____

_____

_____

_____

_____

CHAPTER 2

CHOOSING THE IDEAL METAPHOR: SHIP OF STATE

We are tied to the ocean. And when we go back to the sea,
whether it is to sail or to watch—we are going back whence we came.

–John F. Kennedy

I f we are convinced that our task of understanding our nonprofit organization can be made easier and more rewarding by using a metaphor to describe it, then the subsequent question becomes: What model of metaphor would work best?

An infinite number of possible choices exist, but in my decade-long search in working with nonprofit groups to find the right clarifying metaphor, one consistently powerful and immediately resonant model never fails to move a group's power of imagination and engagement: the great and magisterial, three-masted, squared-rigged, tall ship.

The sailing ship metaphor is powerful and resounds immediately with every group I've ever suggested it to. A huge aspect of its appeal comes from its connection to the enduring sense of journey, since ships are principally designed to be a means of conveyance. Our inborn human need to explore on a planet whose surface is 70 percent aquatic has compelled us to enter the waters in these vessels that enable us to travel to distant lands and discover unknown shores. There's something inherently alluring and daring in taking a journey across water. Since we are land-based creatures, traversing across vast and even forbidding landscapes doesn't compare to the excitement, romance, and hazard of moving across vast expanses of water.

This profound appeal echoes in humanity's rich literary tradition of recounting tales of heroes on their long quests. We read, in Homer's epic, of Odysseus traveling across dangerous seas in his decade-long journey to return home from the Trojan War. We marvel at the challenges that confront Jason and his Argonauts in search of the Golden Fleece. One of America's most compelling novels—Herman Melville's nineteenth-century classic, *Moby Dick*—recounts the obsessed Captain Ahab's hunt for the white whale. But nautical metaphors don't appear only in seafaring classics. The last line of *The Great Gatsby* contains a very famous metaphor: "So we beat on, boats against the current, borne back ceaselessly into the past."

We are equally enamored of true stories of seafaring tales. We relish the tales of those explorers who set sail to find new routes and new lands. We celebrate the heroic and bold determination of Christopher Columbus, who sailed off into what many believed would be his doom but instead encountered the New World. That fascination was refueled fifty years ago as we followed the stories of the world's intrepid new sailors into a new "sea" of space exploration. The "-naut" suffix of the terms astro*naut* and cosmo*naut* reflects that nautical, seafaring metaphor.

People respond to an organizational crisis when the boss explains we need "all hands on deck" because if we're going to "weather this storm" we're going to have to "batten down the hatches."

The ship metaphor also draws its strengths from other aspects beyond travel. If we are to think of our organization as a ship, one of our first concerns is that it be seaworthy. We check to make sure that the hull is watertight so it will protect the crew and cargo. Those who sail on the ship feel a shared sense of connection and responsibility: we're all in this vessel together and our fates feel uniquely bound to one another, especially when the seas turn rough.

When referring to societies as a whole, nautical metaphors have a deep and abiding history. In Book VI of *The Republic*, Plato makes one of the earliest references to a nation as a sailing vessel, a "ship of state." Horace, the Roman poet at the time of Caesar Augustus, employed the same term, referring to his government with a similar metaphor.

Here in this country, we have a rich tradition of embracing the ship metaphor. The USS *Constitution*, known as Old Ironsides, still anchored in Boston Harbor and still listed as an active vessel in the US Navy, floats as a 220-year-old symbol not only of our nautical prowess in the nineteenth century, but also of the nation's endurance. Our literature demonstrates this metaphorical link. In the early days of World War II, both Franklin Roosevelt and Winston Churchill shared a quote from Longfellow's poem *The Building of The Ship* to reassure each of their respective nations to hold steady in the face of Nazi Germany's onslaught against civilization:

> *... sail on, O Ship of State!*
> *Sail on, O UNION, strong and great!*
> *Humanity with all its fears,*
> *With all the hopes of future years,*
> *Is hanging breathless on thy fate!*

The West is far from alone in describing its nation as a ship. The People's Republic of China also invoked the ship of state metaphor in the Cultural Revolution in the 1960s by constant referral to Chairman Mao ZeDong as the "great helmsman" who steered that nation on its revolutionary course.

During that same late-1960s era, for the first time, the inhabitants of Earth saw their planet as a shining blue orb framed against the cold darkness of space, thanks to the pictures taken by NASA's Apollo missions to the moon. These images evoked a global, metaphorical recognition that we are all passengers on Spaceship Earth, sailing in the vast sea of the cosmos. That same spirit of a shared vessel has acted as a catalytic agent in developing a worldwide consciousness of environmentalism.

The organization-as-ship metaphor extends into the domestic political arena as well, especially as national election commentators attempt to depict political motivations as the race for the presidency gains momentum. For example, on the MSNBC program *The Ed Show*, broadcast on December 21, 2011, Democratic House Minority Leader Steny Hoyer (D-MD) complained about what he viewed as Republican attempts to cripple the economy to insure that President Obama would not be re-elected to a second term: "There are a lot of people who are prepared to sink the ship in order to drown the captain." The show's host, Ed Schultz, went on to explain the metaphor for those who may have not understood it: "Drown the captain. Now, who would that captain be? Well, that would be the President of the United States. Sink the ship? That's the country."

President Obama himself has invoked an implied nautical metaphor throughout his administration, referring frequently to "economic headwinds" that challenge the US recovery from the Great Recession.

Again, this suggests the picture of the United States as a sailing ship struggling to move forward despite the daunting external forces of nature—literal winds that push against the ship's direction—that impede its progress.

The President's affinity for this kind of language points to another great advantage of using a nautical metaphor. Such references are clear and easily understood, since they flow from a rich, widely known vocabulary that stays ever present in our day-to-day language. People respond to an organizational crisis when the boss explains we need "all hands on deck" because if we're going to "weather this storm" we're going to have to "batten down the hatches." In wind-tossed economic seas, a business may have to "clear the decks" by "jettisoning some ballast" so the ship can avoid "foundering." In the deepest part of the storm, we may await the dreaded command to "man the lifeboats." And if we do survive the storm, we don't want our organization to be "left high and dry" on some barren coral reef.

Extending the Metaphor to Nonprofit Organizations

If one adopts the metaphorical image of a nonprofit organization as a ship, the next task is to compare all aspects of the nonprofit to its analogous counterpart.

For the balance of this book, each chapter will address and develop a specific aspect of this metaphor to the fullest extent, applying it to a key aspect of a nonprofit organization.

Compass Points

◇ The ship has a great deal of appeal as an organizational metaphor because it taps into our familiarity with vibrant images of journey.

◇ We have a rich, easily summoned vocabulary at our disposal when we start using nautical terms to think and converse metaphorically.

Points to Consider

1. If you were to think of your organization as a ship, what image first comes to mind in terms of its size, condition, and overall seaworthiness?

_____
_____
_____
_____
_____
_____
_____

2. Of all the conditions that you summon up that represent your organizational ship's weaknesses, what are the first things you would likely address to keep your ship from sinking?

_____
_____
_____
_____
_____
_____
_____

CHAPTER 3

THE ULTIMATE DESTINATION:
VISION AND VALUES

*If you want to build a ship, don't drum up people to collect
wood and don't assign them tasks and work, but rather teach
them to long for the immensity of the sea.*

–Antoine de Saint-Exupéry

Visions form the spiritual core of all organizations. Visions articulate the way things will ideally turn out. Ask any for-profit what their vision is, and you will unmistakably hear the one unified, consistent response common to all: to create wealth for our owners.

Nonprofit organizations do not have this same commonality. Each nonprofit has a different and distinct vision about how each of them will bring about a new, idealized future. Every nonprofit has the same quest: seeking a purposeful, profound change from existing conditions. Whether it's a world that is no longer stalked by some deadly disease, or a world in which the environment is cleaner and healthier, a world where war is forsaken, or a city is transformed by creating the finest possible performing arts, a world where animals are treated humanely, or a world where lives are no longer destroyed by addiction, all of these represent noble destinations. Nonprofit organizations are all pilgrims. Their journey is founded upon a purposeful destination. Nonprofit organizations depend upon a dream of a promised change, a voyage, as Tennyson said, "to seek a newer world." These are the promised shorelines that the nonprofit ship sets as its ultimate destination.

Visions act as powerful magnets. A dynamic tension pulls between the opposing poles of what exists now and what could be. To resolve this tension, movement has to occur. Advocates for the ideal future will demand to resolve the pressure by urging that we begin the movement toward that new world, metaphorically describing that undertaking as a journey, pilgrimage, or seagoing embarkation.

When thinking about historic seafaring metaphors, recall that Christopher Columbus had a vision to find a new route to the East Indies that inspired him to embark on his seaborne adventure. Columbus would never have acquired the investment support of the Castilian royal family, allowing him to assemble his modest three-ship fleet, had he not given them a compelling vision of how his journey would pay back their kingdom in endless riches once he established this faster and cheaper route to the East Indies. Similarly, no nonprofit will ever gain the necessary support for its "ship"—neither in forming a board, gathering volunteers, or collecting any funds—if it cannot describe what its ideal destination will look like.

This is the essence of a nonprofit's vision: describing the destination, how the community or world will be transformed. The clarity, persistence, and endless appeal of that ideally described destination create the spark for bringing a nonprofit into being and sustaining it throughout its lifetime.

Visions are articulated dreams. Dr. Martin Luther King, Jr. described his vision of a nation no longer imprisoned by racial intolerance in what became to be known as the "I Have a Dream" speech on August 28, 1963, in front of the Lincoln Memorial. His speech contained the five essential characteristics of a truly forceful vision.

First, a vision must be connected to a deeply held set of values. Dr. King reminded us in that speech that this dream of racial equality was "rooted in the American Dream," founded upon the fundamental belief affirmed in the Declaration of Independence that all people were given the unalienable rights of life, liberty, and the pursuit of happiness.

Second, a vision must be compelling, reinforcing the desire to bring the vision into actuality. Dr. King spoke of the urgency of correcting this great deficit of justice, promises made but not yet kept for black Americans a century after the Civil War. He also assured the nation that this resolution could not be brought about through unlawful means or through violence and hatred.

Third, no vision has value unless it is attainable. Dr. King's speech spoke about the attainable ways in which the nation would be changed: racial inequality would disappear as discrimination became recognized as a true contradiction to American values, swept away by reconnecting with the promise America made to itself when it declared itself free.

Fourth, visions have to be converted into actions; otherwise, they never grow beyond the state of simply being dreams. Here Dr. King described how racial inequality would be translated into political freedom by action—exercising the freedom to vote, and to vote for protecting their rights. He went on to proclaim how this would translate into economic freedom—to no longer be denied access to commercial establishments, to move and live freely in communities as full-fledged citizens.

The fifth and most obvious characteristic that marks a vision is its intense visibility. A true vision evokes a mental image in vivid detail. In the final three minutes of his speech, Dr. King richly described a new America, freed of racial hatred, one where racial harmony was found even in places where one could scarcely ever imagine it occurring. In that short space he repeated the phrase "I have a dream" nine times, each time offering a description of how racial harmony would look in this future America.

Dr. King's speech still resonates within our nation's mind, fifty years later. That's a final tribute to his speech, though it's unlikely he would have known it would have that timeless aspect to it.

Visions are fragile. They fade quickly unless they are told and retold, refreshed, and given the chance to remind people of the ultimate dream that holds them together with hope and determination. For almost two thousand years, Jews have had a rich tradition of refreshing their collective vision of their idealized future at the conclusion of the Seder meal at Passover or at the end of Yom Kippur service, proclaiming, "Next year in Jerusalem."

Visions are the enduring reminders of the final destination. Some very bold visions will journey many generations before reaching their destined ports. That means the vision will pass from the founders (builders) of the ship to their successors over the ages of time. Somehow, the enduring message about what the final destination is to look like must be preserved so the successors can stay on course.

Without knowing what the destination looks like, the ship has no chance of ever knowing if it's getting closer to its Promised Land. This unfortunate nonprofit ship might sail endlessly, never actually recalling its final destination. It may try to raise its sails to catch any prevailing wind—that is, pursue any activities that will attract funding—but its real purpose of trying to reach a destination will never succeed. These aimless nonprofit ships eventually lose all consciousness of why they ever sailed in the first place. The vision has disappeared and so has any idea of a final destination. At this point, the ship turns to a new purpose—to simply keep the ship endlessly afloat. The ship's owners, captain, and crew can all become so enraptured with their own welfare that they can no longer call to mind that they are responsible for delivering their passengers to the ideal (and now forgotten) destination.

Tragically, these nonprofits condemn themselves, their passengers, and their donors to a curse as cruel as that of the legendary Flying Dutchman, the ghost ship condemned to sail the oceans forever, never to find its ultimate destination.

Values

The decision to change the community—or the world—doesn't occur spontaneously. It springs forth from a judgment based on a set of values that are integral to the making of that decision. Values form the subatomic matter that comprises visions.

For example, if a founding group makes a resolution that a deadly disease should be combated—that its victims and families should find some form of collective support, that research should be done to find a cure or a means of prevention—then it has made core value selections, even though its members may not have been aware that those values inspired them. Creating a vision that declares a future without this dread disease means the visionaries hold certain beliefs. One of those fundamental beliefs will be that humankind's fate is not to simply submit to disease, that there are ways to avoid it or eradicate it. A second value would be that in our collective humanity, if any of us suffers, then we all suffer in some way. That belief evokes a response rooted in compassion. Additional values may be found in a deep faith in science in general and medical science in particular.

These principles need to be explicitly written down and proclaimed because they form the fundamental reason for making the visionary destination desirable. In effect, where the vision describes the voyage's ultimate destination, the values explain the compelling reason to construct the ship that will convey us there.

The vision and underlying values represent the fundamental spiritual core of the organization. They are established by the nonprofit founders, and their successors—the future boards of directors—have the obligation to keep these ideals alive and to use the values as the touchstones for determining right actions. It is every board's ultimate duty to continuously proclaim the nonprofit ship's destination, to rouse themselves to action, to alert those passengers who want to board this ship to that ideal destination, and, finally, to encourage support from the public to help fund this noble journey.

This is the essence of a nonprofit's vision: describing the destination, how the community or world will be transformed. Without knowing what the destination looks like, the ship has no chance of ever knowing if it's getting closer to its Promised Land.

Compass Points

✧ A vision statement describes the final destination of the nonprofit ship. It must be clearly stated and preserved.

✧ Values remind the ship's leadership and crew why its founders chose the vision and why both values and vision continue to influence the ship's reason for being.

✧ The board guards and proclaims the vision and values to the community to invite participants and supporters to become involved.

Points to Consider

1. Does your organization have a vision of the ideal world it's trying to create? Describe it in your own words.

_____
_____
_____
_____
_____
_____
_____

2. What values does your organization profess? What does it believe to be fundamentally true? What does it promise to the community it serves? In what principled way does it promise to act?

_____
_____
_____
_____
_____
_____
_____

Power of Vision

The Elm Valley Insurance Cooperative, a nonprofit established to provide basic medical services to those in the community who could not afford such coverage, was established by several major hospitals and clinics. Representatives from each of those dozen health care providers were appointed as the governing board to insure that it was meeting its mission promise.

This was no simple assignment. The downturn in the local economy had demolished thousands of jobs and, with their disappearance, basic health coverage had disappeared for those employees and their families. The board was faced with a quickly rising demand that strained its meager financial reserves. At the next board meeting, they would have to "sharpen their pencils" as the board treasurer put it, indicating significant reductions in program funding were clearly going to be enacted.

The board was comprised of a number of distinguished professionals: a handful of well-regarded physicians, some of whom held prestigious teaching positions with the local university hospital; several highly renowned surgeons; topped off with a sprinkling of consummately competent hospital administrators.

Prior to the board meeting, the board had requested that a morning retreat session be held to refresh their focus on the major issues to be tackled in the coming year (year two, to be exact) of their ongoing strategic plan.

At the initial session of that morning's retreat, the facilitator led off the process with a review of the Cooperative's values and vision statements. As those words scrolled up the screen, the majority of the participants simply stared blankly ahead. "I want to know how you feel about these statements," the facilitator said.

"What are they?" asked Dr. Anastas, reflecting the board's confusion.

"This one, over here, is the vision," the facilitator explained. "*Elm Valley will be a community that provides essential medical care to all citizens who otherwise do not possess the means to access it.* And over here," she pointed to the other side of the PowerPoint slide, "are the founding board's values:

"*We believe that access to basic health care is a fundamental right to every citizen in our community.*

"*We believe that we all have a fundamental responsibility to assure that such care is available.*

"*We pledge to use every creative and compassionate means to create a financially sustainable method to insure that this model of universal health care access protects all our citizens.*"

Dr. Habeeb rubbed his chin in wonder. "Who wrote this?"

The facilitator chimed in, "The founding board set all this in place back in 1993 when the Cooperative was first formed."

"Wow," Dr. Habeeb reflected, "that's pretty amazing. What were they thinking?!"

Dr. Nguyen then spoke up. "Elm Valley was much more prosperous back in that day. The whole nation was. We hardly had anyone who needed this kind of safety net. Things are certainly a lot more challenging now. Thank heavens we established the foundation back then."

"We really need to rethink all this," offered Dr. Lutz, the board treasurer. "The numbers of applicants are killing us these days. We just have to re-tool this whole vision thing—it's way too 'pie in the sky' nowadays. We need to stay very aware of our fiduciary responsibility and keep this enterprise sustainable." Heads nodded all around in general agreement.

"We can address all this in some other session," remarked the board chair. "Let's move on to review our program metrics. See where we can trim away at some of our services." He looked down at his agenda. "What's this part here about participant feedback?"

Rita, the executive director, reminded him, "Remember, at the last board session, the board passed a resolution to open its future meetings with a brief moment for listening to someone who has received our services. You know, they felt it was nice touch, sort of sets the mood, and reminds us of why we exist. Our guest today couldn't be here for the board meeting later this afternoon, but she could stop by this morning. So I thought we'd have her speak at the kick-off of our retreat."

The board chair blinked and sighed. "Sure. OK, show her in."

Rita rose and brought in a young woman, who was accompanied by her five-year-old son, Isaiah. She introduced herself and her son, speaking just above a loud whisper. She was clearly anxious standing in the presence of all these scions of the medical community. "I want to thank you all for your very good medical help your organization provided for my son." She continued somewhat hesitantly while Isaiah stood by, squirming slightly, but beaming a huge smile as he looked around at the board. "I mean, Isaiah—he—would not be here"—at this moment her voice cracked as she choked back a sob—"if you had not treated him so quickly." The young mother was able to murmur something like, "And I'll never forget—" and then came the tears. Rita jumped up to comfort her. Isaiah continued to charm everyone with his big smile. Rita thanked her and hustled them both out to the anteroom.

The board stayed silent for the next twenty seconds until Rita came back into the room. "Sorry," she apologized. "She's fine. Just got a bit emotional."

"Look," began Dr. Anastas, clearing his throat as discreetly as he could, "I'd like to suggest that we move with a little more consideration on the task ahead this morning. I'm sure we can direct more of our creative focus toward looking for more resources rather than becoming too drastic about service cuts."

CHAPTER 4

THE SHIPBUILDERS:
THE FOUNDERS

*Never be afraid to try something new. Remember that a lone amateur
built the Ark. A large group of professionals built the* Titanic.

—*Dave Barry*

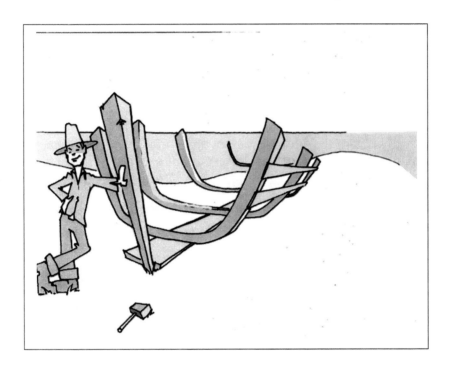

W hen thinking of the most famous shipbuilder, it's hard to summon up a bigger name than the Old Testament figure, Noah. Divinely inspired, Noah set upon an epic undertaking, one that he pursued diligently and, in some accounts, carried on despite the derision and criticism of those who thought him quite mad.

The founder's role in the nonprofit world will often be marked by similar themes. Driven by what *could* be rather than what is, founders act contrary to the conventionally accepted status quo. Founders act once they have decided that conditions once considered "unfortunate" need to be regarded as unacceptable. At that transformative moment, everything can change.

Many people experience this at an individual level. For instance, one day a woman wakes up and decides that she is no longer going to be a hostage to a smoking habit. A young man rouses to the realization that he can rise above what others have claimed to be his station in life.

People are inspired to change more than just their own lives. Every day, in thousands of communities, people ponder a vision to re-shape the future. Those individuals become motivated by any number of compelling notions: Our city's river shore can be transformed from this industrial dump into a major park. We don't have to answer violence with violence. We can find a way to understand and conquer a disease. Our city can become a mecca for this form of unique art for which we have been recognized.

To be successful, founders have to inspire others to see the possibilities of this newly envisioned world. Aligning these others with their vision and shared values, they set about building the great ship that will take the community to the new future. Many of these close early allies will be among the founding board of directors. As explained in chapter 7, this and all successive boards are always the "moral" owners of the ship.

Over the expanse of time, the ship's founder will often choose to continue the journey in a new role. After serving originally as one of the collective owners on the board, the founder will be appointed by the board to the position of executive director and will now serve as the ship's first captain (executive director, see chapter 8). This new role puts the founder into a very detailed and tactical leadership role, one that demands great management skills and business acumen.

> To be successful, founders have to inspire others to see the possibilities of this newly envisioned world.

Many founders go through this transition to spend years in distinguished service. As founders they are adept in the role of explaining the nonprofit's vision, convincing others to support their organizations. In their leadership roles, the founders can inspire people to come aboard as part of the crew (staff, see chapter 8). These founder/captains (executive directors) become legendary faces of their organizations. After a successful career, they may again be invited to return to an honorary position on the board, in the role of a member emeritus, available to give the governing board wisdom, encouragement, and insight into the organization's deep memory and values.

Of course, many nonprofits go on to serve communities for generations, long outliving the founder. Still, the legends of the founder can help support the organization. Having someone who can still recall being a witness to the creation of the organization, evoke the founder's zeal, and tell the heroic stories of overcoming the early challenges keeps the founder alive in a spiritual way, which helps strengthen the resolve of owners, captain, and crew.

Instances exist, however, when the founder's legacy and success do not endure. One can see a similar syndrome in the for-profit arena, where many start-up entrepreneurs can be very successful, but then find they do not have the right skills, knowledge, or temperament to translate their garage-based enterprise into a larger one. The skills necessary to found an organization may be completely unusable in actually running it. Nonprofit founders can fall victim to this same vulnerability. Sometimes the founder's ego, enlarged by overcoming so many challenges and obstacles in building the ship, interferes with her good judgment. This syndrome will manifest in these kinds of behaviors:

- **Failure to manage crew (staff).** The founder's history will often be characterized by a great deal of self-reliance, heroic behavior. No other person has been so dedicated, selfless, or tireless in getting the organization formed. A founder's strengths may not translate at all into sound management judgment. As the ship gets larger and more crew is added, the founder has to become more adept at management. It is one thing to command a small tugboat, quite another to lead a towering, four-masted tall ship. The result: a potentially under-utilized or mismanaged staff, a founder/executive director headed for burnout, and a ship that's adrift.

- **Ignoring the ship's owners (board).** The founder very likely was a major influence in bringing all these members onto the board. While they can be credited with being early supporters of the mission and vision, they won't have the same importance in the founder's eyes as she who founded the organization. The founder remains skeptical of the board's collective wisdom and its grasp of the organization's real needs. The founder resents the board as an intrusive and at times even illegitimate force that wants to interfere with the ship's direction. As the executive director, a strongly determined founder can sometimes over-dominate the board, using threats of resigning and taking her talents and goodwill with her. The result: an ungoverned ship, the owners (board) subservient to the captain, no force to counterbalance or improve the founder-captain's perception and strategic judgment.

A pernicious form of founder's syndrome can blend all of these symptoms into a toxic brew that compounds the dangers of both: a ship that is badly managed with little chance of remedying that situation since the ship's owners have been frozen by fear and don't dare to confront the founder.

All of these dangers can be avoided as long as the ship's owners (board members) remain steadfast in their role as supreme authority and responsible agents for the ship's success. Founder or not, the executive director (captain) always serves under the board's command

and oversight. The board must stay aware of the founder's management capabilities, evaluating her performance on a regular basis. It should not stand simply in the role of critic, but also offer ways to enhance the founder/executive director's management skills, through education or management counseling advice.

Above all, both the ship owners and captain/founder must adopt a guiding principle that mission success transcends everything. While it certainly will be true that the founder created the ship, the ship still sails only to deliver the passengers to the promised envisioned shore, not as an expression of the greater glory of the founder.

Compass Points

◇ The founders play a key role in creating the ship and its early success.
◇ Founders often transition successfully to become executive directors (captains).
◇ Founders may struggle to meet the challenges of the captain's role.
◇ The board is obliged to help the founder succeed in that role, but if it proves beyond the founder's ability, the board must act to find competent talent to fill that role.

Points to Consider

1. Tell the story of your organization's creation and founder. What role did the founder go on to play? If that person still abides with the ship, in what way does the founder currently add value?

_____

_____

_____

_____

_____

_____

_____

2. Assuming your founder still plays a role in the organization, in what ways can the board help in his/her success?

_____

_____

_____

_____

_____

_____

_____

3. If your organization has been in existence long enough to have outlived the founder, what remains of the original values and vision? Does anyone still serve in the organization who recalls the founder and shares the story of the organization's first struggles and triumphs? What value might you derive from such a recollection?

_____

_____

_____

_____

_____

_____

_____

4. How would you describe your board's involvement in asking potential investors for funding? How might you increase its participation rate in bringing in resources?

_____

_____

_____

_____

_____

_____

_____

Sinking the Ship He Built

Leonard, the board chair, joined the conference call with the other members of the executive committee just a few minutes late. "Sorry," he offered, "I'm between planes and it took me a bit to find a quiet spot here in the airport to call in. Anyway, I appreciate all of you agreeing to this emergency call."

Then he launched into the substance of the session. "Look, the financials for our academy are tanking fast and the operational report is littered with all sorts of very grim indicators. I know the board session is over two weeks away, but we have to act soon based on what I have to say is an evolving crisis."

The rest of the group knew he was saying what everyone felt. The academy was careening out of control. The number of enrolled students had declined this semester, following the resignation of several key respected teachers. A major grant they were all counting on would not be delivered, since their in-house development director suddenly quit last week.

And none of this made any sense. In the six years since its founding, the school had made huge strides in its enrollment and students' academic success. People flocked to get their children enrolled in the New Academy and its revolutionary teaching approach created by Reginald, the Academy's founder. In its early days, Reginald had enlisted a number of his closest friends, all teachers, into this bold, experimental primary grade school.

As the visionary founder, Reginald had started this nonprofit school, assembled a board of directors from academics and personal friends, taught his fledgling faculty in his methods, and did all the major fundraising to acquire the capital to get the school established. Within the first year of its operation, the board appointed Reginald to the position of Head of School. It seemed a perfect move.

Success soon built upon success. The school seemed to have a found the magic elixir to motivating disadvantaged students to reach higher and higher realms of academic achievement. Even the national media spotlight swung around to showcase this upstart academy on its third anniversary, the envy of every public school in the state, when a brief interview with Reginald on National Public Radio was followed 12 months later with a very favorable CBS *60 Minutes* segment.

After that, Reginald was swept into the national speaking circuit. He was in demand everywhere. He was even among two dozen people the White House invited to participate in a retreat on creative solutions for national education policy, held at Camp David. His positive notoriety accelerated the Academy's brand, and enrollment surged.

Reginald came back from that conference and pressed the board to adopt an aggressive building campaign.

"We should anticipate a 30 percent annual growth rate over the next decade," he claimed.

The board, which had grown in membership since its founding but still included only people whom Reginald personally approved, was taken aback by this bold assertion. But, they reasoned, what did they know? After all, Reginald had been hobnobbing with the President and the Secretary of Education at Camp David just last week.

This was all followed by an aggressive capital campaign, which met 80 percent of its goal. Reginald convinced the board to allow the Academy to sign a note for the remaining 20 percent. "Sure as the sun will rise tomorrow, payoff will occur in less than a year!" he assured the board.

Although the sun did rise the next day and continued to do so faithfully for the next year, the payoff did not meet that schedule. In fact, the Academy was now in its third year of struggling to find money to meet those payments. Growth was not 30 percent as Reginald predicted. It had begun to level off at 10 percent in the second year and then slowed to even less the next. Predicted revenues never materialized, putting off the debt repayment long into the future. But that was only one dimension of the problems the Academy faced.

Reginald had expanded his faculty and staff to meet the anticipated swelling enrollment. Though he did continue to coach the new teachers in his methods, his relationship with them was not the same as with his original crew. They did not implicitly trust him. They hadn't been his friends, as the first wave of faculty had been. Many challenged some of his methodologies, something Reginald would not tolerate as his public image and ego continued to grow.

As the school grew in complexity and demanded more hands-on management, Reginald was seen less and less on campus. He delighted in going on his national speaking tours, which did, one had to admit, help build the Academy's brand and attract potential grant money. In his absence, however, he left no one with real authority to address issues. Whenever Reginald returned, he undermined whatever his temporary appointee had decided. It didn't take long for the faculty and staff to become more and more anxious and dispirited.

The financial pressures forced some cash flow problems that led to missing two successive payroll obligations. Reginald, having no business acumen, could not figure out a financial strategy to resolve this crisis. Several faculty members, outraged by this incompetence, resigned. Staff confidence in his leadership plummeted, especially among the new faculty. Word on the street was that the Academy was in danger of closing, causing some people to withdraw their students.

"OK," said Leonard," what are we going to do?"

Karla, the board treasurer, was the first to speak. "We've got to get Reginald some kind of management and financial expertise to help him make some key decisions and I mean fast. He seems incapable of handling this crisis."

"I agree," responded Chuck, the board secretary and the member with the longest board service among the conference callers, "He's way, way out of his depth. I heard that he almost had a breakdown at the last faculty meeting, shouting about how they were all betraying him. Then he stormed out for the rest of the day. I worry about his health."

Simone, the Vice-Chair, was more direct. "I think we should replace him."

Leonard pushed back. "This is his Academy, based on his unique, successful method. I can't imagine we'd last a year without his participation in developing his method. No, if we lose him, the whole ship sinks."

"In case you haven't noticed," Simone shot back, "this ship is already listing badly in the water. If we keep this incompetent in command, the ship will sink. Maybe we don't have to remove him entirely. Maybe we just need to get him out of this management position."

Chuck jumped in at this point. "That might work. If we kept Reginald on as a creative consultant, someone who could be the person who advocates for the school, but remove him from his dreadful role of operating the school, maybe we can save the Academy that way."

Leonard was skeptical. "Reginald's got a bit of an ego on him. He's unlikely to want to have something like this look like a demotion. We'd have to make the title sound like a real advancement."

Simone countered, "Listen, just because he built this ship doesn't mean he has the exclusive right to scuttle it. We are the agents responsible for keeping this vessel afloat. There's no way he's going to meet any of the performance measures we forged with him in his review process. Let's advise him that we're open to exploring various ways in which he can continue to serve, but in this role as it is currently designed, his day has passed."

Leonard reflected on Simone's proposal and then asked," What about just getting some management and financial consultants in to help him manage better?"

Chuck interrupted before Simone could reply. "Leonard, we don't have that kind of time to see if Reginald will listen and change his behavior based on that counseling. We'd better act decisively, and now. Even if Reginald resigns and walks away, we still have a fighting chance to keep his method alive in our Academy culture. That's the legacy we want to preserve to help our students succeed."

"OK," replied Leonard, "let's draft this proposal to change his role and plan to call the board into emergency session. I'll schedule an appointment with Reginald to update him on our concerns and what we're thinking. We've got to act."

CHAPTER 5

PROPELLING THE SHIP: MISSION AND PROGRAMS

One ship drives East, and one drives West,
By the selfsame wind that blows;
It's the set of the sails, and not the gales,
Which determines the way it goes.

— *Ella Wheeler Wilcox,* Winds of Fate

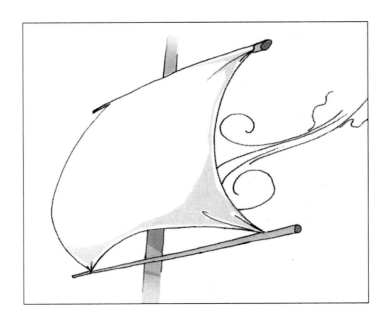

T he whole purpose of a ship is conveyance. That occurs by harnessing some form of energy. A ship can take advantage of the propulsion power of the surface currents upon which it glides, or the transformation of sheer human muscle power into rowing, or it can capture the power of the wind in great expanses of canvas sails, or harness the converted power of coal, oil, or nuclear energy to fire up the engines that turn the ship's underwater propellers.

A nonprofit's vision identifies its destination. The mission defines what the ship must do to arrive there. If *visionaries* see and describe the end destination and, through that process, inspire people to sail towards it, then it becomes the work of *missionaries* to ensure that the ship is powered and navigates its way toward that promised shore.

On the nonprofit ship, the programs—or activities—it engages in to achieve the mission represent our metaphorical ship's means of propulsion through the waters.

For example, the American Heart Association (AHA) has a proclaimed this as its mission: "to build healthier lives, free of cardiovascular disease and stroke." Its dream, or vision, will be a world where no one suffers any longer from these mortal diseases (heart disease is the number-one killer in the U.S.; strokes rank fourth).

How does the AHA propose to build these healthier lives that will be free of these dread diseases? Though not articulated in their mission statement, the AHA describes in its annual report three specific ways, or programs, by which it pursues mission success: (1) funding innovative research; (2) fighting for stronger public health policies; and (3) providing lifesaving tools and information to prevent and treat these diseases. These are the three major engines (or sails, in keeping with the tall ship image) that propel the AHA ship toward its vision.

In order to maintain its course, to ensure that its engines are running true (or that its sails are full of wind) and the ship is moving faithfully on course toward that envisioned shore, it requires some form of clear measurements. At the detailed level of its annual report, the AHA describes the many program activities that will occur: the research to be conducted and reported, the advocacy for healthier public policies at local, state, and federal levels, the educational forums they will conduct, and expanded access to health services for all.

Each of these actions consumes resources, results in observable and measureable activities, and can be tallied into long columns of data representing the total amount of work being performed. Labeled in the nonprofit field as "outputs," for the AHA these include research papers published, people trained, number and diversity of populations given health care access, and public policies enacted. Yet, by themselves, all these indicators are not enough to tell if the ship is moving toward the targeted shore. These measurements are the equivalent of recording how many piston strokes have occurred in the engine room, revolutions per minute of the propellers, or the extent to which the canvas sails strain with the fullness of the wind.

The captain and crew (executive director and staff, see chapter 8) and certainly the owners (board of directors, see chapter 7) and passengers (ultimate stakeholders or those people the mission serves, see chapter 6) need much more assurance of progress than that. The real payoff comes from measuring the resultant changes in people's behaviors and health. As a consequence of the research, then, what new methods, treatments, or medications will come forth to save lives? As policies are enacted, how do they reduce unhealthy behaviors and decrease conditions such as the population's obesity rate which, in turn, reduces cardiovascular disease? As people become educated, to what extent do they take up new, healthy habits, such as exercise, and thereby diminish their risk for stroke and heart attack?

In other words, what are the measurable larger outcomes from all this activity that show that the AHA is really making a difference?

The AHA has responded to this question by setting its strategic navigational gauges "to improve the cardiovascular health of all Americans by 20 percent while reducing deaths from cardiovascular diseases and stroke by 20 percent, all by the year 2020." Unlike the more tactical actions and measures, these goals represent significant and strategic goals indicating the ship's promised progress toward that ultimate, visionary destination: a world without cardiovascular disease.

The number and types of programs the organization will want to maintain will change over time depending on the needs of the community. There will be opportunities for growth. As the nonprofit ship expands the number of people it serves (passengers it takes on board), the ship has to increase its size. But it also has to increase its ability to move that larger vessel, which means increasing the capacity of its programs—its means of propulsion (engines, oars, or sails).

Careful consideration has to be given when a nonprofit wants to augment its program (engine) inventory. For example, a ship may be very comfortable with a set of programs that it has developed over time. Perhaps they were sustained through annual donations and were simple to operate. In time, however, a new program may be offered that might be more sophisticated. That new engine, so to speak, might require more resources, or more staff. This may be analogous to converting from a sail-powered ship to one that has an internal engine. That conversion can represent a significant change in the needed crew as well as the overhead operating expenses. The challenge will be to manage those new overhead costs and see if that new engine produces the added benefit to the stakeholders (passengers).

Augmenting the ship's propulsion power by adding sails or engines represents only one aspect. There are instances as well where the ship should consider dismantling some of the old propulsion engines or sails. For example, a program that may have been used in the early stages of the organization may no longer be of real use to the ship because its passengers no longer require it; that particular program no longer helps propel the ship in the right direction. In this case, it's appropriate to say that it's time to dismantle that engine and perhaps replace it with one that serves the passengers better and therefore propels the ship in a more faithful direction.

There are other instances that affect whether or not certain programs should be maintained. During difficult economic times, the nonprofit ship may have to scale itself back simply to stay afloat financially. It may have to shrink the size of the ship, allow fewer passengers to board, release some crew members, and cut back on the costs of running all the engines (programs).

If *visionaries* see and describe the end destination and, through that process, inspire people to sail towards it, then it becomes the work of *missionaries* to ensure that the ship is powered and navigates its way toward that promised shore.

The question then arises: Who has the responsibility to decide which new programs to put into place, which to jettison, or which to augment? While the actual management of the programs falls to the captain and crew (executive director and staff), the ultimate determination of whether or not to keep these particular engines in place, changed or otherwise, falls to the ship's owners (board). While the board should consult the captain and crew about the details and metrics involved in evaluating the effectiveness of these programs, the board's ultimate decision rests upon discerning whether or not those programs are producing true evidence of making a difference in people's lives. In other words, do these programs actually help propel the ship towards the ultimate envisioned destination? Realize that it can be difficult to make this determination because many programs will *seem* to be productive. Seeing pistons pulsating and the propellers turning does not necessarily mean the ship is going in the right direction. This is symptomatic of a lot of "busyness" but not real forward movement.

Compass Points

- Vision is about the destination itself, while mission is about the forward movement towards that destination.
- A ship has to propel itself towards the destination; in this metaphor, the propelling engines are *programs.*
- A nonprofit adds, augments, and occasionally dismantles programs over time in response to community needs.
- Some program changes require added staff expertise and overhead expense, similar to converting from a sail to an internal combustion engine on a ship.
- Programs should be evaluated periodically by the board to ensure that they do in fact provide forward motion towards the destination (demonstrate outcomes).

1. Write out in this space your ship's mission statement. To what extent do you believe this statement represents a clear and concise description of what your organization promises to do to reach its ultimate destination?

_____

_____

_____

_____

_____

_____

2. List your major programs. How is each one measured in terms of its effectiveness in moving the ship towards its ultimate destination (outcomes)?

_____

_____

_____

_____

_____

_____

_____

3. Describe the means and method by which the board of directors periodically reviews the programs. What history do you have in adding, augmenting, or eliminating programs?

_____

_____

_____

_____

_____

_____

_____

4. Describe an instance where a change in your organization's programs caused the need for additional staff, expertise, or other needs.

_____
_____
_____
_____
_____
_____
_____
_____

5. Describe the methods your organization uses to ensure that programs are run effectively and efficiently.

_____
_____
_____
_____
_____
_____
_____

Dinner with the Trustees

As the dinner plates were being cleared and the board of trustees was preparing to go into its quarterly session, the president and deans of Foghorn University were setting up their PowerPoint presentations.

The atmosphere was relaxed, filled with the comfortable bonhomie that was normally present at these rather inconsequential sessions. Much like a ritual fire dance, the university's president and his academic leadership had prepared the standard-issue series of messages that they knew would keep the board of trustees reassured that all was well.

What they were not counting on, however, was Sonja. Sonja was a new addition to the board. She had served in other trustee roles and had recently been schooled in the nuances of nonprofit mission measurement principles. One of her intentions was to test whether or not the data she was about to hear would indicate whether the University was in fact succeeding in its mission.

The board chair introduced the university president, who then stepped up to the podium and began his presentation to the full board of trustees. The first slide showed a picture of the university campus with the mission statement emblazoned across the top. "Foghorn University is dedicated to the mission of educating its students to become leaders of tomorrow in the world."

The president then walked the board through a series of slides where he described the new endowment, showed pictures of new buildings that were being constructed on the campus, mentioned the university football team's recent successful bowl game, and displayed graduation rates for both undergraduate and graduate programs. The statistics showed that the number of degrees granted was increasing slowly year by year. The deans of the various schools had been able to adhere to their budgets. There was encouraging news in the medical school, which had successfully landed a National Institutes of Health grant on cancer research.

The board of trustees sat silently and respectfully through the presentation. A few had begun to nod off, challenged by digesting a very large dinner just before the slide show began. When the president had finished his performance he asked the obligatory, "Are there any questions?"

A few moments passed and the president was about to turn the meeting back over to the board chair when Sonja raised her hand and asked, "Excuse me, but can you tell me if the university is succeeding in its mission?"

The president paused and, looking a bit taken aback, replied, "Well— yes, certainly."

The president, still a bit unnerved by this impertinence, tried to smile and said, "I believe the past dozen slides have shown ample evidence of our success."

Sonja replied, "I have no doubt that the slides show that the university has had a lot of activity going on during the past quarter, but I don't see how any of that necessarily shows that we're being successful."

The other trustees began to shift uncomfortably in their chairs. Alfred, a trustee emeritus, entered into the conversation at this point. "Our new trustee here should be forgiven, since she is new and doesn't understand how we have traditionally gauged the university's progress."

Sonja turned toward Alfred and replied, "Quite the contrary. I think I do understand how you have measured success, and I don't think it has anything to do with understanding whether or not you're achieving your mission."

Constance, the new board of trustees chairperson, then entered the conversation by asking Sonja, "What would you suggest that we use as a means of making that determination?"

Sonja, not missing a beat, quickly responded, "I'd like to know more about the accomplishments of the people who graduated from the university. Our mission says that we produce people who become leaders in the world. So what is our evidence of these leaders' accomplishments? Do we have any statistics about how our graduates have demonstrated this leadership in the communities where they live?"

A few moments of silence ensued as people reflected on what Sonja had just said. Then Constance remarked, "I don't believe we have the wherewithal to make that kind of measurement." The other board members nodded in agreement.

The vice chair, Oscar, offered his opinion. "I suppose you could say that we have evidence of our success every time we feature one of our alumni in our quarterly magazine."

Sonja picked up on that idea and nodded in agreement, adding, "That's precisely what I am talking about. However, we graduate 300 people every year from our various colleges and have done this for over 70 years. Through our quarterly alumni publication, we establish evidence of having four people whom we can claim are successful representatives of succeeding in our mission. It just makes me wonder what other impact our graduates are having as leaders in the world."

Constance offered another observation. "You know of course that we have one of the highest rates of alumni contributions to our endowment compared with other regional colleges. That certainly is evidence of our graduates' success."

Sonja thought for a moment and then responded, "That certainly can be an encouraging sign. It does perhaps demonstrate that some of our graduates are economically successful. But that's not the entire picture, is it? I hope that their economic success is grounded in the virtues and principles that we tried to teach them while they were here on campus. I would be disconcerted if we were graduating people who went on to a life of generating wealth without somehow knowing they were achieving it in ennobling ways."

Now the room was really starting to buzz with conversation. Constance had to gavel the group back to order.

Sonja continued, "Please, I know that I'm new here and it is not my intention to stir up ill will, but I believe that we can become too distracted by activities such as winning athletic recognition or grinding out diplomas from year to year. Our founders certainly expected that we would be educating people to become leaders. Perhaps we are, but I think we're becoming sidetracked with data that distract our attention from measuring the important things."

Constance had to gavel the group back to order once more. While there was no time at the current board meeting to pursue this conversation any further, Constance did entertain a motion from one of the other trustees to establish an ad hoc committee to look into how the trustees could consider a higher-order level-of-outcomes measurement to ensure that the university was, in fact, achieving its mission. The motion was seconded and the committee was established. Sonja graciously offered to chair that committee, saying that she would be happy to meet with any of the trustees to further the conversation on how they might gather information about graduates and their lifelong accomplishments in order to help the university understand that it was truly achieving its promise.

CHAPTER 6

THE PASSENGERS: THOSE SERVED BY THE MISSION

We travel together, passengers on a little spaceship, dependent on its vulnerable reserves of air and soil, all committed, for our safety, to its security and peace.

–Adlai Stevenson

T he whole reason for the ship's existence, its functions, its very reason to make this journey, is to deliver the passengers safely to their promised port. The passengers represent the nonprofit's primary stakeholders, the ones for whom the founder(s) promised a new future.

The stakeholders may be as vast as all of humankind if the mission, for example, is a universal one such as bringing an end to world hunger. Or the stakeholders may be as small as a group of homeowners within a few square blocks where a neighborhood association has pledged to recapture the area from gang violence and drugs. It is simply a matter of scale. The most important thing, however, remains in knowing who the passengers are, what their particular needs are, and ensuring that everything the ship does is focused upon delivering them to that idealized, promised destination (the vision, see chapter 3).

Some nonprofits are bound on a journey which will deliver all their passengers to the envisioned shore at the same time. In the earlier example, the neighborhood association whose focus is to improve the living conditions in a small neighborhood area might be able to substantially achieve that goal for all residents in a manner of a few short years. All the residents would then enjoy the benefits of improved safety, order, and comfortable surroundings at more or less the same time.

Other nonprofits, however, might have much more ambitious plans, plans that are focused upon making worldwide changes. In these cases, the passengers (all of humankind) will eventually get there, some perhaps sooner than others.

Here's a historic example. When the March of Dimes was founded in the mid-1930s to eradicate polio, the founders knew that they would someday deliver the entire world to a new shore where polio no longer threatened humanity. When, less than twenty years from the organization's founding, the Salk vaccine had been developed, ambitious inoculation programs spread rapidly in the Western world. The March of Dimes had begun to deliver the first of us on the planet to that new destination, forever free of polio. In the ensuing sixty years since the Salk vaccine was created, the last vestiges of people who still need inoculation exist in small, isolated pockets of Asia and Africa. Newer nonprofits with missions similar to the March of Dimes' original vision are now dedicated to finishing the job. Their aim is to deliver the last of humankind from the plague of the polio virus.

Sometimes it can appear to be very easy to identify the passengers. One may say, for example, that the passengers on one particular nonprofit ship are those who have been promised to be delivered from drug addiction. The promised shore to which the ship owners (board of directors, see chapter 8), captain and crew (executive director and staff, see chapter 7) have pledged to deliver those passengers is one upon which the passengers will find their lives freed from that dependency.

But take this concept even one step further. Even among the primary beneficiaries of the mission focus—those who are trying to free themselves of their drug dependency—there may be important differences. Some may be focused on defeating alcohol as their main challenge. Others, however, may be seeking a way to overcome addiction to other substances, the treatments for which may be substantially different.

Whether because the ship's passengers may have significant secondary needs, or because the promises made to these passengers may also affect a wider circle of people, the point is this: the ship's passengers are not always a homogeneous group. They may represent different classes of passengers, not because of social privilege or status, but because of the subtle differences of their needs and the organization's promised outcomes.

> The ship's passengers' needs can change over time, affecting the very mission itself.

Beyond those primary passengers who are directly served by the mission, there may in fact be other passengers (stakeholders) who benefit indirectly from the mission's success. In the above example about people being freed from addiction, one can easily recognize that the families of those recovering from that dependency also represent a group of stakeholders. It is easy to see how the families of the addicted yearn for that same promised shore that represents a new life and hope for their recovered family member. So in this instance, one could argue that there are two different classes of passengers with slight variations in needs, still generally united by the mission and vision of the nonprofit ship that is conveying them.

The ship's passengers' needs can change over time, affecting the very mission itself. For example, imagine a nonprofit that was set up in the 1890s to address the needs of the poor. The causes and resultant remedies of what constituted poverty in that community in that century may have had a very pronounced descriptive focus. Presume that same agency still exists today. For that ship's owners (board of directors), the questions become:

- How does poverty manifest itself in this, the twenty-first century?
- In what ways is it similar to the nineteenth-century model?
- In what ways has its manifestation changed?
- How might poverty be expressed in new and telling ways that were not present 120 years ago?
- How does that affect how we identify our passengers?

Another key factor in considering those being served also encompasses the total geographic scope of those who are to be served. The number of passengers a nonprofit feels it can bring on board its ship is a key determinant of the organization's mission and the scope of its promised effect. An example of this can be found where a nonprofit that has traditionally served the community in one geographic part of the city decides to expand its coverage to include a larger geographic swath of the city. In making this decision, the organization is essentially saying that the ship wants to be able to take on more passengers. This opens up a whole host of other questions such as the amount of resources it might take to serve a wider and more diverse population of potential passengers. The issue of scalability becomes vitally important. A nonprofit, for example, may be able to serve twice as many people as it currently does for the same per capita cost that it did in the past with a smaller population. However, at some point the number of people being served will approach certain thresholds which will change that per capita cost. It will also affect the overall revenue consumption as the organization grows to accommodate more passengers. This calculation leads into the question of expanding the size of the ship to serve more people. This, in turn, opens further investigation into the ship's need to increase its financial base.

Compass Points

- ◇ The whole purpose of the nonprofit ship is to serve its stakeholders (passengers) by delivering them to their promised destination.
- ◇ Passengers are not necessarily one amorphous group. While all of them are beneficiaries of the mission, they may have varying needs that need to be addressed.
- ◇ The scope of the nonprofit's purpose and promise determines how many passengers it proposes to carry; this directly affects the revenue and resources needed by the nonprofit to succeed.

Points to Consider

1. Describe your primary passengers—the ones most directly served by your mission.

_____

_____

_____

_____

_____

_____

_____

2. How might your passengers (stakeholders) be segmented into distinct subgroups? Define how their needs may vary. How does this affect your mission?

_____

_____

_____

_____

_____

_____

_____

3. Describe how your ship delivers its passengers to the envisioned port. Do you plan to deliver them all at once, or is this going to be a gradual delivery of passengers over time?

_____

_____

_____

_____

_____

_____

Passenger Levels

The United States Association of Professional Ukulele Players (USAPUP) began its annual member conference as scheduled on a bright spring day in Honolulu. This year's record-breaking attendance was marked by a spirit of deep dissatisfaction with the organization's board of directors. As the board chair gaveled the first plenary session to order early in the morning of the first day of the conference, the members started clamoring for extended time to be recognized by the board panel to hear their comments.

Harry, a long-term member, demanded to know why the board had failed in one of its prime objectives during this past year. He charged that the board's strategic promise to promote the art of ukulele playing to a point that the United States would embrace it as much as it had done in the 1920s was a miserable failure. He railed on and on about how there were no stories in the national media about the art of ukulele playing, or the joy that it brings, or the therapeutic effects it has on both listeners and players.

Ogden, a relatively new member of the association, voiced a different complaint. He felt that the art and skill of playing the ukulele was soon to die out altogether if the association failed to recruit new members more aggressively from the millennial and Gen X youth of America. That comment was countered by Seymour, a lifelong member of the association, who bitterly complained that the association would doom the time-honored, traditional sound of the ukulele if they allowed those younger players in.

Seymour clearly despised the younger players' "punk-uke" genre, an absolute abomination of the art, he claimed.

Edna represented the provisional wing of the conservative uke players. During her allowed public forum time with the board at the plenary session, she pressed for a resolution saying that the cheap plastic ukuleles that many uke players preferred should be officially disapproved by the association.

The last speaker from the floor asked for the association to publicly endorse the superiority of the smaller, traditional tenor uke over the larger and less orthodox baritone uke. This suggestion provoked a large outcry from the baritone uke players who began throwing their souvenir conference ukulele picks at the speaker.

Later in the evening at the formal board session, Olaf, the retiring board chair, presided over the board's discussion on trying to meet the association members' wants and needs.

For over ninety minutes the conversation reeled wildly out of control, caroming off one issue after another, allowing everyone to vent but resolving nothing. Finally, Daisy June, the newly elected chair, took command of the conversation. "Listen," she insisted, "we're never going to get anywhere until we lock in on several basic answers. Now, the very first one is this: What is our mission?"

Lattimore, the board's secretary, offered his faithfully memorized recitation: "The United States Association of Professional Ukulele Players promotes fellowship, entertainment, performance, and education among ukulele enthusiasts all across the US of A!" Everyone applauded his enthusiastic and accurate pronouncement.

"Super!" exclaimed Daisy June. "And now, Lattimore, can you also tell us what USAPUP's vision is?"

Once again Lattimore did not disappoint. "We envision a world where all people who want to learn, play, and entertain others with the melodious sounds of the ukulele will have the opportunity to do so and, through that form of music, make the world a more joyful place." Cheers erupted once again all around the table.

"Now, ladies and gentlemen, "Daisy June pressed on, "whom do you think we serve, based on those statements you just heard Lattimore so eloquently proclaim?"

Many responses followed. "Uke players!" "Uke enthusiasts!" "Anybody who enjoys uke music!"

Daisy June beamed at the enlivened group. "Who do you think is right?"

Olaf commented, "I think they all are."

Everyone nodded in agreement. Daisy June continued, "Our membership is made up of all these different types: some who play the uke—amateurs through professionals—and others who just love to listen to uke music. We also have people who make ukuleles both in traditional forms and unique materials, and many who experiment with new kinds of music on the uke. But they all are united by the love of the instrument itself and the art of its music.

"Now, we heard a lot of fussing and feuding at today's session from those who feel passionate about their uke issues and aren't afraid to speak at this kind of forum. But when was the last time we actually canvassed our membership about what they really want us to do as an association?"

75

No one seemed to have any recollection of doing that in at least a decade. "Sounds like we need to make that a priority, then," Daisy June suggested. "And, Clarence," she directed her attention to the chair of the membership committee, "I know that you've been working on our membership trends. How are we doing with our membership numbers?"

Clarence shuffled through his membership folder and pulled out the summary page he had just completed before attending the conference. "It looks to me like we're in our fifth year of slow decline. We've lost 5 to 7 percent of our membership every year since 2007."

Board officers all began to frown at this news. Daisy June then asked, "Do we know why these folks are abandoning the ship?"

Clarence shook his head. "No, we don't ask anything when people leave. But I do hear lots of people say they would prefer to join their state ukulele associations."

Daisy continued, "Do we keep any statistics about our members that might help us better understand what we're doing right or wrong?"

Clarence looked down through the various columns of his report containing membership data. He noticed that they did capture the age of each of the members. Clarence did some quick calculations and said, "I can see that the average age of our members is around fifty-seven years old."

Daisy June gasped at that statistic. The board members looked equally surprised.

"I'd say that we are quite literally becoming extinct," remarked Ogden. "I recall when I joined the organization twenty years ago that there were a lot more young people, including me," he smiled, "that made up this organization."

Lattimore rejoined the conversation at this point. "So we've got a membership in decline and aging. We have no idea why, and the only time we speak to our members with any real purpose is at this annual conference. And that always seems to degrade into nothing but one long gripe session that leads to no particular action. We do know from those sessions that our members have had varying concerns and differences of opinion. If we don't turn this around somehow, we will go extinct, and why shouldn't we?"

Daisy June took the floor once more. "It's becoming clear we have a lot of diverse needs among our members, and they're voting with their feet, so to speak, because we're not meeting their needs. We don't even really understand what their needs are. The only people who are showing any devotion to staying on board with us might just be here through force of habit. We owe it to ourselves and to our members to get a better grasp of how we can serve them and see if we can't turn this ship in the direction that we've always promised to our members."

CHAPTER 7

THE SHIP'S OWNERS:
THE BOARD OF DIRECTORS

Tis skill, not strength, that governs a ship.

–Thomas Fuller

T he board of directors for a large, for-profit cruise line convened its regular quarterly meeting. The board chair, Mr. Blaine, began the session by reminding the board that their ultimate responsibility was to exercise their best business judgment and to act in a way that they reasonably believed to be in the best interests of their shareholders, or owners. Going over the quarterly financial reports, the board discussed the financial results, compared them to the expected shareholder return on investment, and pronounced themselves pleased with the cruise line's progress. They later reviewed the strategy that outlined the addition of a new super cruise ship, one that promised even higher profits during the next three-year period. Having finished all items on the agenda, and feeling quite pleased with the major indicators of success from a shareholder perspective, the meeting came to a close.

In the for-profit world, the shareholders expect their representatives on the board to act on their behalf to increase their shareholder wealth. In the nonprofit world, the stakeholders rely upon this same set of representatives to ensure that they benefit from the mission.

That special classification of representation and responsibility in both for-profit and nonprofit realms resides with the board of directors.

In the nonprofit world, the board is legally responsible for the organization. They are considered the "moral" owners of the organization's vision. The board owns the ultimate authority and accountability for the nonprofit's success. In most cases, nonprofit boards of directors are not elected or appointed by those whom they serve. They come to that responsibility as volunteers pledging their ultimate accountability to ensuring that the mission does succeed.

In our nautical metaphor, the board represents the ship's owners. In a manner similar to the opening anecdote about the cruise line's board of directors, the nonprofit board holds in sacred trust the pledge "to exercise their best business judgment to act in a way that they reasonably believe to be in the best interests of their *stakeholders*" through assuring that the organization moves toward its mission's success.

This means that the board will ensure that the nonprofit ship will be strong enough, large enough, financially sound, competently managed, and headed in the proper direction so that its passengers (stakeholders) will ultimately be delivered to their promised port (vision).

In both the for-profit and nonprofit realms, that promise can be betrayed. Consider the colossal board-governance failures that led to the collapse of Enron in 2001, WorldCom in 2003, and Lehman Brothers in 2008. In each of these cases, the board of directors—the ones who were pledged to be the watchdogs, to assure their shareholders that the organizations were being competently and responsibly managed—failed miserably in their duties. There is even some evidence to suggest that some of the board members colluded with top managers in their criminal betrayal of stockholders' interests. The calamitous result of this governance failure was the complete loss of all shareholder wealth.

In a similar way, it is possible to witness a nonprofit board betraying its stakeholders. A board that completely ignores its financial oversight responsibility can stand idly by while the organization's resources are substantially drained away though embezzlement, fraud, or total mismanagement. It can refuse to lift a finger to help bring in resources as the organization drowns in a sea of debt. It can pay no attention to the condition of the stakeholders, not caring if they are really being helped. It can remain willfully ignorant of activities that are violating law, dishonoring donor intentions, or harming stakeholders.

> The board owns the ultimate authority and accountability for the nonprofit's success.

In other words, the owners do nothing to keep the ship from sinking, not caring about the effect it may have on the passengers.

Perhaps none of these failures will ever get the nationwide publicity that the massive for-profit failures receive, but the catastrophic results that can be visited upon the stakeholders by these disreputable boards is still tragic.

In the case of all nonprofits, boards govern. Their responsibility covers a wide swath of activities. As the ship's owners, they provide general oversight of the finances, establish the strategic direction of the organization, set policies in place, and are active in seeing to it that adequate resources are available to support the organization. All of this is aimed at ensuring mission success.

Some nonprofits eventually grow to the point where they have the resources to employ paid staff. In these nonprofits, the board appoints, supports, and evaluates the chief management officer, the executive director. That individual manages the rest of the staff.

Reviewing the nautical metaphor at this point, we have this series of relationships: The board of directors (owners) is responsible to the stakeholders (passengers). The board appoints a captain (executive director), who commands the ship, and who, in turn, hires and manages a crew (staff and volunteers, see chapter 8), all of whom are in charge of running their respective parts of the ship properly.

One of the key questions in this metaphorical application is whether the board (owners) should have a regular presence on a ship that is commanded by its appointed captain and run by a capable crew. It would certainly be expected that the board would be familiar with the ship, would visit it on occasion, and would be able to generally understand its size, shape, and operational capabilities. However, the board would not normally ride with the ship on a continuing basis. By turning over the ship's general management to the executive director (captain), the board should feel that it is not necessary for them to sail on the vessel with the passengers and crew.

Some boards may feel they should take up permanent residence on the ship as part of their role of supporting the captain and crew. There are a lot of downsides to this ongoing presence. A board that insists upon remaining that deeply engaged with the ship and its operations diminishes its crucial governing capability. Board members that wander about the ship on a continuous basis are very likely to assume behaviors that make them appear to be the last and highest level of management. This attitude will bring about a contentious relationship with the captain. They will continuously challenge the captain's decisions and authority.

Even more troubling, if a board decides to maintain its presence on the ship, it will very likely compromise its strategic view. Boards become distracted by tactical observations. They worry about the occasional piston pings they hear in the engine room. That leads to the temptation to go down there and "help" the engine room mechanics. Such assistance could be helpful, but boards that become engaged in that kind of minutiae will soon no longer have time to perform their actual governance role.

The board that remains on the ship will only be able to perceive things tactically, limiting its view to what it can see from the bridge of the ship, an identical perspective to what the captain can see, but with no more helpful insight.

The real added value of a board's viewpoint can be compared to the high, strategic view of the weather systems that the world has come to rely upon from the satellites employed by the National Oceanic and Atmospheric Administration. Those "eyes in the sky" have the capability of viewing the vast expanses of entire oceans. That perspective has critically improved weather forecasting accuracy.

As a vital component of its governing value, a board should take on a similar role. The board must take a satellite view. They provide a perspective that the captain and crew simply can never hope to have from the ship's railing. The board, when it fully activates its strategic perspective, will foresee and warn about gathering storms, or bring key insightful perspective about the proper position of the ship relative to the promised destination that can often elude people who are ship-bound.

As the adage goes, "Two heads are better than one." So, too, does the board enjoy a special advantage as a group charged with assuring that the ship sails safely toward its promised destination. The ship's owners amplify their value when they enlist a variety of members with expert and distinct viewpoints to be numbered among them. This gives the owners a chance to reflect on issues, inviting different views, alternate solutions, and creative approaches to understanding how to ensure the ship's success.

Aside from being dedicated to the passengers' safe passage to the promised destination, the ship's owners also owe loyalty to one another. This does not mean they can't disagree. In fact, no board should count itself healthy if it never witnesses a stirring debate or conflict over policy or strategic questions. High-functioning boards can endure spirited debate, allow contending voices to be heard, and then impartially move to a final decision without shredding their fundamental trust and regard for one another. Once the group comes to a decision, all board members are obligated to unify themselves behind it, clearly giving one voice to their will.

Compass Points

✧ The board of directors is the "moral" owner of the nonprofit ship, ultimately responsible to the passengers.

✧ The board, as the ship's owner, needs to understand the changing needs of its passengers.

✧ A key value the board brings to the ship is its strategic perspective that it gives to the captain and crew.

✧ The board benefits from diverse points of view and healthy dialogue, and then unifies itself in its final decision.

Points to Consider

1. Describe the ways in which your board acts as responsible owners of the mission and ultimate promise (vision).

_____
_____
_____
_____
_____
_____
_____

2. How might your board improve upon its understanding of the passengers' (stakeholders') changing needs?

_____

_____

_____

_____

_____

_____

_____

3. How does your board offer its strategic view to help the captain and crew better ensure mission success?

_____

_____

_____

_____

_____

_____

_____

The Board Steps In

The board sat in session, discussing how it could be of service to the big, annual holiday season party for Save Our Youth. With less than a month to go, plans were well underway to prepare for the organization's primary fundraising event. This event also celebrated all the teens who had completed their training in the Save Our Youth outreach programs. These young people came from neighborhoods where they had very little opportunity to learn social skills and potential job skills that could lead to better lives.

Throughout the evening, awards were given to several of those outstanding youth members who demonstrated remarkable changes in their dedication in pursuit of gaining these new skills.

The board was going over its list of potential assignments with Henry, the executive director. They checked off which board members would be greeters, who would act as hosts, who would act as MC, who would act as food servers. It was heartening to see how the board eagerly anticipated trading their governing roles for those of much more humbling service. But as they thought of it, it really was all part of the same fabric. They were all volunteers, after all, and they were all there to serve. At the gala, service was just more visibly demonstrated.

As Henry went over more of the details, he remarked that he had tried to save some money this year by not hiring buses to bring in the youth members. Instead, he explained, he had lined up a number of drivers who would be glad to carpool the teens to the gala and back home.

Irene, the board chair, asked Henry a quick question regarding that idea. "Henry, are those drivers part of our regular volunteer group?"

Henry paused for a second, looked through his planning sheets, and then said, "It seems like seven of the fifteen are. The rest are various family members related to the kids who I recruited."

Irene turned to the other board members and asked, "What does our volunteer policy say about this kind of activity?"

Lucy, the board secretary, found the policy and scanned it quickly. "I don't see any mention about vehicles or drivers. But this is just for one night. I don't know if they even qualify technically as volunteers."

Irene then redirected herself to the rest of the board. "How do the rest of you feel about this? Is this a policy matter?" For the next twenty minutes the board members got into one of their very familiar, spirited debates. Some contended it was not a worry for the board, a tactical matter only for one evening. The more conservative wing of the board felt strongly that the drivers fell well into the scope of the volunteer policy's intent, despite their proposed one-night-only service. As such, they argued, these drivers need to go through the background-check process. The other side pushed back, saying that requirement would cost more than renting the bus service.

Finally, Lucille suggested a compromise. "We've already got seven approved volunteers on the drivers list. Can't we convince just eight more volunteers to drive that evening? That way, we save on bus rental and we protect our youth members at the same time."

Her solution met with resounding support. The board directed Henry to release the eight non-volunteers from driving and recruit eight approved volunteers to fill those vacancies. He dutifully nodded and wrote himself a note on his sheaf of planning papers.

Three weeks later, the gala celebration had a record crowd and raised its second-highest annual contribution total ever. As the board members remained after the big party, helping to sweep up, put chairs back into the closets, and bag the garbage, Irene asked Henry if the board's insistence on having approved volunteers had caused any excessive stress, in addition to all he had to organize.

Henry smiled, "No, not that much, really. Actually, after the board conversation, I did a little informal background checking on my own. Nothing official—just asking around the neighborhood. Turns out two of those people on my original list had suspended driving licenses. One of them was involved in an accident just last week. I think you guys may have helped save us all sorts of potential trouble."

Irene took a deep breath and nodded. "Trouble? No, I think we dodged a major disaster. OK. I think we'll update that volunteer policy ASAP."

CHAPTER 8

THE CAPTAIN AND CREW: EXECUTIVE DIRECTOR, STAFF, AND VOLUNTEERS

O Captain! My Captain! our fearful trip is done
The ship has weather'd every rack, the prize we sought is won

–Walt Whitman

I n 1865, just after Lincoln's assassination, Walt Whitman captured America's grief in his poem, *O Captain, My Captain!* In that work, he metaphorically represents the slain president as the captain of the ship that has just successfully reached its port, a reference to Lincoln's leading the Union to victory in the Civil War, only to suffer martyrdom as soon as the war was concluded.

This metaphor is a very clear reference, easily understood by anyone put into a leadership position. It's an archetypal role, and it summons up a bounty of remembrance of both fictional and nonfictional captains whose stories of command resonate with everyone. The British honor their own Lord Nelson, the brilliant naval commander and brave hero of Trafalgar, where he crushed Napoleon's fleet only to lose his own life in that encounter. Americans have similar heroic captains held in equal reverence, too. There is, for example, Captain James Lawrence, who, as he lay mortally wounded during a naval engagement with the British in the War of 1812, whispered his dying words: "Don't give up the ship."

World literature has given us other memorable examples of captains, some heroic, some very flawed. For thirty years, British novelist C.S. Forester wrote novels detailing the exploits of his nineteenth-century naval commander Captain Horatio Hornblower. French author Jules Verne created his Captain Nemo in *Twenty Thousand Leagues Under the Sea*. Herman Melville immortalized the monomaniacal Captain Ahab in *Moby Dick*.

The movies and TV have continued this rich tradition of both heroic and deeply disturbed captains. From *Mutiny on the Bounty's* dreaded

Captain Bligh, to *Star Wars'* iconoclastic loner, Han Solo, to *Pirates of the Caribbean's* loony Captain Jack Sparrow, the role of the captain with its challenges and the protagonist's ability to meet them or not are ever present.

Given all of these images and references, it's quite easy to picture the executive director as the captain of the nonprofit ship. The ship's owners (board of directors) define the captain's role, responsibilities, and boundaries of authority. These owners recruit and select the captain to command the ship. The captain reports to and serves at the pleasure of the owners, following their general direction and faithfully bringing the board's collective will into operational reality. Working with the captain, the board develops measureable performance expectations for the immediate future. The board then periodically reviews the captain's performance, supports the captain's endeavors in professional growth, and offers clear, guiding feedback.

The captain is allowed a strong, significant influence upon the board. Most nonprofit captains have a formal position on the board with the ship's owners. This allows the captain and board a somewhat more collegial interrelationship than simply one of boss and subordinate.

The executive director, as captain of the nonprofit ship, has traditionally been assigned responsibilities of both leadership and management to ensure that the ship successfully delivers its passengers to the promised destination.

In the all-important management role, the captain has five essential functions: plan, organize, command, communicate, and control.

Planning

The captain works with the board of directors in formulating the overall strategic direction of the ship (see chapter 7). A key aspect of the captain's role results in translating the overall strategic plans into tactical ones. For example, the board may promulgate a strategy with the purpose of expanding the nonprofit's social media presence in the community over the next several years. It will be up to the captain to develop specific action plans, describing how, when, where, and at what cost that strategy will be translated into action involving such areas as Facebook, Twitter, and other yet-to-be-developed social media.

The planning process never ends. Assumptions and circumstances that undergird an original plan can shift, moved by either internal or external conditions. That signifies continuous adaptation and adjustment, altering the original plan.

Organizing

Moving from planning to action requires organizing resources. The captain will have to create the internal organizational structure and define roles, responsibilities, and relationships. This function also determines resource and work distribution. The captain defines the appropriate departments and draws up and delegates the limits of authority and responsibility.

Commanding

The captain issues the orders to be followed, using the established channels of reporting relationships. Some commands become standing, routine orders. Others find their origin in deliberations over specific circumstances that require the captain's consideration and decision. Depending on the captain's preference, this may or may not involve consulting with subordinates before moving to the command decision point.

Communicating

Management is impossible without clear, frequent, and unambiguous communication between the captain and subordinate team. Communication keeps the vital information needed to assure a well-functioning operation on track. It is absolutely essential in coordinating activities among interacting departments. Effective communication builds confidence, competence, and social trust. Managers typically spend most of their time communicating with others.

Controlling

One of the oldest adages of management focuses on control: "If you aren't measuring it, you're not managing it." Controlling means setting standards, limits, and thresholds of expectation, then measuring, evaluating, and reporting actual results. After the evaluation, management then determines if any necessary corrective action is required. These potential adjustments involve creative problem solving.

Leadership

The captain's job calls for leadership, a wholly different set of characteristics and skills when compared with management.

Managers concentrate on maintaining stability; leaders challenge the status quo. Managers concentrate on work getting accomplished; leaders focus on people becoming developed. Managers derive their power from formal authority; leaders are awarded power through their charisma. Managers abhor risks; leaders take them. Managers center their actions on control; leaders are centered on passion. Managers set rules and boundaries; leaders break through them. Managers avoid conflict; leaders use it. Managers have subordinates; leaders have followers. Managers crave consistency; leaders encourage creativity. Managers do things right; leaders do the right thing.

Despite the contradictions between these two roles, they should be successfully blended into the nonprofit captain's persona as complementary characteristics. There will be times that the ship needs the captain to be more manager than leader, ensuring, for example, that the budgets are being balanced and that quality assurance levels are being achieved. There will be other times, however, when the captain will be called upon to lead, to take bold, creative risks—to propose, for instance, to take on a vexing community issue that no one else will address, that may upset the Establishment wisdom, but which nonetheless is mission-consistent and the right thing to do.

As a consequence of exhibiting these leadership characteristics, the nonprofit ship's captain becomes identified with the ship by the public. The captain's role in speaking out on issues relevant to the ship's mission, publically appealing for financial support, representing the ship in public forums, developing relationships and speaking with the media outlets, all serve to blend, in the general community's mind, the nonprofit with the captain in his leadership role.

The captain's relationship with the owners (board) represents the most compelling predictor of the ship's ability to succeed. A healthy relationship is characterized by clear, honest, and authentic communication between the captain and the owners, generally channeled by the board's chairperson. The healthy relationship stays vibrant when both sides know and respect one another's roles, responsibilities, and boundaries.

The Crew

The nonprofit ship often needs more than a captain on board to set sail and deliver the passengers to the ultimate destination. Having more hands on deck requires recruiting more people to help operate the ship successfully. It is the captain's prerogative to select and direct all these others, subject to the budget allowances and the owners' recruitment and management policies. These potential crewmembers generally fall into one of three categories: paid staff, independent contractors, or volunteers.

The paid staff members are considered employees of the nonprofit. They are subject to the same laws, regulations, and human resource policies established by the ship's owners (board) that address hiring, fair treatment, and dismissal. They all fall under the command of the ship's captain. They should be properly apprised of their authority and responsibility through written job descriptions. They deserve to be given measurable and accountable work to be accomplished and the resources to complete their work assignments successfully. They deserve periodic reviews on their performance and opportunities for developing their performance skills. If the ship's crew grows to an appropriate level of people, the captain might well establish sections with departmental management positions, distributing the captain's authority down a chain of command.

Independent contractors are compensated for their contracted work but are not formal members of the ship's crew. The captain maintains the relationships with those individuals and assigns work under formal, specific agreements. The ship's owners will normally establish a set of policies to guide the captain in the selection and management of these relationships.

Volunteers augment the crew, bringing vast additional talent. Once again, however, the owners establish policies regarding the vetting, selection, management, training, and dismissal of these additional, valued human resources. The captain enacts management principles to ensure the policies are followed. The volunteer force falls under the captain's supervision and leadership.

The crew represents a critical factor in the ship's success. An incompetent crew will drive up costs, retard progress, and can even cause the ship to sink. A masterful, dedicated crew can help the ship get to the promised destination, at times even in the face of dreadful management, poor leadership, or an anesthetized group of owners.

Once again, the captain proves to be a key ingredient to the crew's success. The captain's management and leadership skills will prove to be the most telling factor in getting the crew to perform at their highest potential. The ship's owners do need to oversee the captain's performance in this critical realm, ensuring faithful adherence to human resources policies. Beyond that point, the ship's owners should stay aware of high-level indicators of crew satisfaction. One of the key gauges the owners should monitor is crew turnover rates, particularly in the paid staff. Turnover represents a troubling condition, if for no other reason than because it drives up costs enormously, entailing repeated recruitment and training expenses. But it can also be a danger signal that the captain and crew's relationship is in a chronic state of disruption, something that must be investigated and resolved.

The executive director, as captain of the nonprofit ship, has traditionally been assigned responsibilities of both leadership and management to ensure that the ship successfully delivers its passengers to the promised destination. The captain's relationship with the owners (board) represents the most compelling predictor of the ship's ability to succeed.

The captain of the nonprofit ship represents such a vital lynchpin: the conversion point between governance and management, the interconnecting bridge between the owners and crew, and the public face of the organization, promoting its cause and engendering goodwill on its behalf. For all these reasons, the ship owners have a supreme responsibility to select the most capable person for this role.

The owners can become easily enraptured with a very capable, charismatic, and competent captain. Even with this resounding success, there lurks a very real danger. The owners may be lulled into a sense that this strong-performing individual may stay forever. And many do—for decades, all for the good. Yet the owners' chief responsibility to the passengers also mandates addressing the certain eventuality that the captain must pass along the baton of leadership someday. It may come through a scheduled retirement or, more likely, through an unforeseen circumstance. Therefore, the owners need to ensure that they adopt a comprehensive succession policy so that someone can take the helm if the captain is suddenly removed. No ship can survive the journey for long without someone in command.

Compass Points

◇ The ship's captain is appointed by and responsible to the owners (board) to bring policy and strategic intent into reality.

◇ Successful captains are able to blend the right interplay of leadership and management skills to fulfill their role.

◇ The crew is recruited by and reports to the captain, following the policies regarding recruitment and management set by the owners.

◇ The owners need to ensure that the key role of captain is always supported by a strong succession plan.

Points to Consider

1. Describe your ship's captain's role and responsibilities.

_____

_____

_____

_____

_____

_____

_____

2. What blend of leadership and management have you witnessed in your captain's performance?

_____
_____
_____
_____
_____
_____
_____
_____

3. Describe how your owners address setting the captain's performance expectations and evaluations.

_____
_____
_____
_____
_____
_____
_____
_____

4. Describe your crew's make-up in terms of hired staff, contractors, and volunteers. How effective is each group in its performance?

_____

_____

_____

_____

_____

_____

_____

5. Describe your board's current succession plan and policy. How does it address both short-term and permanent replacement of the executive director?

_____

_____

_____

_____

_____

_____

_____

Succession

The call came at 5:30 in the morning. Chester bolted upright in bed, rousing himself into consciousness. He knew the call had to be bad news, probably from family. As soon as he mumbled hello, the voice at the other end of the line asked, "Is this Mr. Roley?"

Chester didn't recognize the caller, and he felt a brief moment of relief. "Maybe no one in the family has died," he thought. "Yes, this is Mr. Roley," he whispered, trying not to wake his wife.

"Mr. Roley," the quiet voice continued, "This is Virginia, at the Pennington House," she continued.

"Who?!" Chester replied, thinking it might be a wrong number, but realizing it couldn't be, since they seemed to know his name. "I don't know anyone by that name," he went on, preparing to end this disruptive moment.

"No, sir, this is the Pennington House, you know, the halfway house for substance-abuse addicts. You're the chairman of the board there."

Chester was still trying to make sense of this call. "I'm the vice-chair. Lorna Thornberry is the chair."

Virginia persisted, "Mr. Roley, Lorna's term expired thirty days ago. She said you're the new chair."

Chester was still stirring, trying to orient himself. Why is this woman telling me this at this hour? he thought.

"OK, then, thanks for reminding me. But you can't be calling just for that reason," he said, failing to hide his exasperation.

106

"Oh no, Mr. Roley," Virginia continued, "I'm calling because our executive director, Ellen, was in a very serious automobile accident last night. She's in critical condition at St. Vitus hospital."

"Oh, dear God," Chester blurted out, "I'm terribly sorry to hear that. Is there anything I can do?"

"Actually, yes," Virginia continued, "she was supposed to meet with the Bradley Foundation today to answer their final questions on this big grant we're counting on. We want to know if you can go in her place."

Chester was dumbstruck. What did he know about this organization? Next to nothing! He'd only been on the board for a couple of years now and hadn't been clever enough to avoid getting himself nominated in the line of succession to head the board. He'd never even been to the Pennington House itself, since all the board meetings were held in the community room at a bank downtown.

"That's just not possible," Chester stammered. "I mean, why can't you go? Or maybe one of the other staff people?"

Virginia explained, "I'm just a nurse here, Mr. Roley. I don't know anything about the grant-writing business. Besides, I have to be on-site today because state regulations require a medical professional to be here during the day. All the rest of the staff are volunteers or contractors who know even less than I do about grants. And Ellen told us at Monday's staff meeting that this grant deal is a make-or-break proposition for us. That's why, when I got the emergency call last night from our shift manager about Ellen's accident, I started calling board members to see if they could help."

Chester still was in shock. His mind raced to think this through. Ellen had been executive director for, what—12 years or so. She knew everything. Did everything. Didn't they have other people working who could take over? What kind of—suddenly it struck him. Last year's board meeting—that new guy who just joined, talking about the board needing a succession plan for Ellen, how vulnerable the organization was, no contingencies, Ellen being actually too independent, not wanting to share anything she knew with anyone. Chester and the rest of the board knew she'd always be there. She'd helped found the place. Loved everything about it. And it was superb—she'd brought it out of absolutely nothing into a well-respected treatment center for young addicts, had a national social work magazine praise her treatment model, won some awards, attracted new grant money. Made the board's job real easy—just had to follow her lead—one of the reasons he joined, he reflected. Well, that, and because he had a favorite nephew who had needed help and had his life turned around at Pennington House. Chester thought it would be a nice gesture to show his thanks and support by joining the board.

"Now what?" he pondered. No telling how long Ellen would be out of commission or if she would ever be able to return to her leadership role. How would the organization be able to survive? It sounded like this grant hearing was critical. But even if they got past that, how would Pennington House get by? How would they recruit? Did Ellen even have a job description? Did the board have any idea of how to advertise, interview, select for this position? And what would all of this cost? He couldn't recall what their last budget report reflected.

Then Chester suddenly felt the full weight of the burden falling on his shoulders. What about those young adults who were relying on Pennington House to help them recover? What about their lives?

CHAPTER 9

BOUNDARIES: OWNERS, CAPTAIN, CREW, AND PASSENGERS

Do not worry about holding high position;
worry rather about playing your proper role.

–Confucius

Sophie's cell phone started buzzing insistently during her early-morning staff meeting. She could sense its low-frequency vibrations deep inside her purse. "I'll get it later," she thought, even though she had a good idea who the caller was. Sure enough, after her morning meeting she checked her messages and there they were: two different staff members at the Hopewell House had attempted to get in contact with her.

Sophie, as board chair, wondered why she had taken on this responsibility, since it seemed to bring on endless challenges. When she returned the calls, she found the same general complaints that she had heard the week before. The staff was upset with the executive director. Ernst wasn't being fair, complained one; he kept assigning overtime to Bernice, instead of her. Stefan, the other staff member who had called, thought Ernst was being a little too abrupt in his conversational tone lately and he wanted the board chair to know of his dissatisfaction.

"Okay, okay, I give up," Sophie thought. "I might as well go ahead now with my weekly call to Ernst and try to straighten him out. I never would have taken this board chair role if I had known it involved this much work."

The conversation did not go well. It never did. Ernst had become more and more defensive and resentful over these calls. His management authority was continuously compromised by a staff member's complaining calls to the board, followed by a reprimanding directive from the board chair. He contested this board "intrusion on his turf," as he called it.

The board leadership disagreed. They had a long tradition of this behavior. But they were growing weary of trying to break in executive directors to do their will. After five executive directors in five years, you'd think they'd finally find the right candidate. Perhaps the next one would be more compliant.

Among the most challenging aspects of commanding the nonprofit enterprise is defining relationship boundaries. The less certainty over how the board, executive director, and staff/volunteers are supposed to act in concert with one another, the more chaos will reign.

As illustrated in the earlier chapters, all three of these major areas have distinctive, complementary, vital roles to play in bringing about mission success. Coupling these components in a precise and unambiguous manner is of critical importance.

Here's the essential breakdown of who plays what role, using our maritime metaphorical model.

Passengers: Stakeholders, for whom the mission brings ultimate benefit. They are the reason for building the ship and taking the journey.

Owners: The board of directors, representing and accountable to all of the passengers to whom they have promised safe and sure passage to the final destination.

Captain: The executive director, appointed by the board, responsible and accountable to the board, following their broad, general, and collective demand to manage the ship efficiently and successfully so that the passengers reach the promised destination.

Crew: The staff, hired by, responsible, and accountable to the executive director. These individuals perform various roles within the ship to ensure that the passengers are delivered to the ultimate destination.

There are six possible, paired relationships among these four categories:

1. Passengers and Owners

2. Passengers and Captain

3. Passengers and Crew

4. Owners and Captain

5. Owners and Crew

6. Captain and Crew

In each of these relationships, we can describe the range of healthy, appropriate interactions as well as the ones that are unsuitable and even destructive.

(1) Passengers and Owners (Stakeholders and Board)

Most nonprofit boards serve as the unelected representative advocates for the stakeholders. They may be self-selected or nominated by other board members, but none of this dims their ultimate accountability to the stakeholders. The board should, as a consequence of this solemn devotion, possess some essential knowledge about the stakeholders and their needs. They do not have to be experts, but at minimum, they should be conversant with their overall needs and how the organization should respond strategically. To ensure that stakeholders' interests are always in view, some boards embed into the by-laws that some minimum number of board members be actual stakeholders. For example, a nonprofit that has a mission to fight a certain disease might require a certain number of people who suffer from that disease to be board members.

Among the most challenging aspects of commanding the nonprofit enterprise is defining relationship boundaries. The less certainty over how the board, executive director, and staff/volunteers are supposed to act in concert with one another, the more chaos will reign.

Dysfunction in the passenger-owner relationship can manifest itself in two major ways. The first occurs when the owners have no understanding or knowledge of passenger needs. The owners just assume that all is well. They remain willfully uninformed regarding passenger satisfaction or desires. They see that responsibility as something the captain and crew should own. In this dysfunction, the passengers represent a mere abstraction in the owners' minds. For example, one will witness this problem when the board of a food bank remains clueless about trends in a community's increasing poverty rate occasioned by a regional recession and the dramatic increase in hunger that will result.

At the other end of the spectrum, the opposite dysfunction expresses itself in the owners' hyper-intrusion into accommodating the passengers' needs. In this instance, the owners become distracted from their strategic oversight role and endlessly interfere with the captain and crew's day-to-day operations. An example of this kind of over-involvement can be found in the story of a board's relentless engagement with its soup kitchen's operations. Rather than setting a policy in place guiding the executive director around issues about food quality and balanced nutrition, this hyper-involved board continuously wants to advise about food preparation activities. This only reinforces, in a wholly different way, the negative effects of too many cooks spoiling the broth.

Example: Board members engaged in serving meals in the homeless shelter become distracted with the fact that the food is not tasty enough. The strategic issue might justifiably be food acquisition and quality, but the board could become over-engaged on recipe preferences.

(2) Passengers and Captain
(Stakeholders and Executive Director)

The captain of the ship has a primary responsibility to ensure that the passengers are safe and responsibly delivered to their promised destination. This means the captain will often have a much deeper understanding of stakeholder needs than the owners (board). The captain has to see to it that the board's strategic wishes are translated into effective, supporting, tactical actions. This demands particular attention to details, engaging in solid management practices. In very large organizations, with a large crew, the captain may have very limited time to spend directly with stakeholders, but that should not diminish the executive director's requirement to have a strong, comprehensive understanding of how their needs are being addressed.

Example: The captain regularly reviews program metrics and finds time to meet with passengers (stakeholders). No issue is too tactical for the captain to consider and then turn over to the right crew member to resolve.

The dysfunctional relationship between the captain and passengers can occur if the captain spends too much of his/her time with the passengers and interferes with crew responsibilities. This behavior not only leads to crew resentment, but it also depletes the time the captain needs to spend leading and managing the crew.

(3) Passengers and Crew (Stakeholders and Staff)

These two groups have a close working relationship. The crew (staff) provides the essential services directly to the passengers (stakeholders). The crew stays engaged at a very tactical level, taking care of the detailed programmatic services assigned to them by the captain. The crew justifiably has the most comprehensive understanding of stakeholder needs. The crew also has responsibility for faithfully following the directions of the captain in their day-to-day responsibilities.

Example: The staff in a food bank ensures that food is properly collected, catalogued, stored, and distributed according to proper policies and procedures.

Dysfunction between these two groups can arise if the crew (staff) loses its focus on providing the highest-quality service to the passengers. It

118

can also occur if the staff loses its authentic concern for the well-being of the stakeholders. Nothing can be as damaging as seeing a staff treat the stakeholders as inconsequential objects.

(4) Owners and Captain (Board and Executive Director)

This relationship is one of the most critical in the entire nonprofit ship. The connection between these two entities represents the interconnection between governance and management. The board has responsibility for establishing the strategic direction and policies to be followed. The executive director (captain) is responsible for turning that plan into reality through strong management and at the same time putting into effect procedures that follow the general policy guidelines established by the board.

No matter how many crew members may be hired, the captain remains the sole direct employee of the board. The board provides general oversight and reviews the captain's performance on an annual basis. Working in collegiality with the captain, the owners will also set annual performance goals and expectations that form the basis of an annual performance review.

The captain, when finances allow, is given the authority to hire and supervise (and, if necessary, fire) the crew members. All of the human resource decisions the captain makes must be in accordance with the overall human resource management policies that the board puts in place.

The relationship between the captain and the owners depends upon a great deal of clear and frequent communication and on developing a strong sense of trust between the overseeing authorities and the person responsible for fulfilling the collective will of the board of directors (owners).

Example: The board reviews programs for their effectiveness and, working with the captain, suggests that a new program be developed. The captain, working with his crew, proposes that new program to the board. The board considers that program and, upon approving it, directs the captain to bring it to reality within the limits of certain time frames and budget considerations. Then, on a periodic basis, the captain reports back to the board on the program's progress.

A dysfunctional relationship can occur when the captain is given no real authority to implement the strategic plan. A very constricting oversight board can severely limit the captain's authority or demand to review and approve every decision, no matter how inconsequential. In this case, the board considers itself the last official and highest level of management, rather than an overseeing, governing body.

(5) Owners and Crew (The Board and the Staff)

Because the executive director represents a layer between the board (owners) and the crew (staff), there exists a delicate and nuanced circumstance when considering the relationship between the owners and crew. In order to maintain a very important concept in management called "unity of command," it's important to remember that the owners' will should be expressed to the captain, who in turn sees to it that the crew complies.

Direct communication and interactions between the owners (board) and the crew (staff) needs to follow a specific and orderly protocol. Normal communications should flow between those entities through the captain. This is not to say that there aren't proper instances where the staff would be working directly with the board members. Oftentimes crew members are invited to be present at board meetings and can be called upon to brief the board on certain issues.

As a rule, individual board members should not be contacting the crew members without prior clearance and approval from the captain. In addition, the staff should refrain from directly contacting the board without similar approval from the captain. There will be instances, however, where individual board members and staff members will be called upon to work together without the specific presence of the captain. This normally occurs within the confines of board committees which are often populated by both board members and staff members. Staff (crew) members are normally assigned to those committees to help the committee with information and details to which the board (owners) otherwise would not have access.

Example: An ad hoc committee to study program outputs and outcomes is established by the board. The executive director (captain) agrees to have her program directors attend those committee meetings. Those particular program directors help the assigned board members on that committee understand the data and help assemble the recommendations to the board. In this instance, those crew members (staff) on the committee have been given full approval by their immediate supervisor, backed by the captain (executive director), to work directly with those board members. Those staff members (crew) may be given additional assignments by the committee chair, who will typically be a board member, and that additional work will be authorized by the captain (executive director).

A dysfunctional example can be found when an individual board member calls up a staff member to request specific work or information without prior knowledge or approval for that inquiry from the captain (executive director). This violation of the chain of command represents an end-run around the authority of the executive director (captain). It confuses and conflicts the crew (staff) member as to who has the proper authority to assign priority crew work.

(6) Captain and Crew (Executive Director and Staff)

This relationship is one of the clearest to describe. It represents the most traditional form of management structure. The captain (executive director) has full authority and responsibility for providing general overall command of the crew, who should respond by executing their assigned responsibilities and fulfilling clearly established expectations. The captain not only manages but also leads through modeling the way, encouraging the staff to give their best effort in support of the mission, offering opportunities for professional development, rewarding their progress, and encouraging them to succeed.

Dysfunction in this relationship can occur through poor management or leadership on the part of the captain or in instances when a staff (crew) member fails to respond or tries to subvert the captain's legitimate authority through means similar to the anecdote at the beginning of this chapter.

There will be instances where these very practical and orderly boundaries might have to be crossed in order to bring stability to an organization that is in some form of crisis. One of the most common of these instances is where the executive director has failed in some way to effectively manage and lead the crew.

There will be justifiable circumstances that compel the board to intervene into the management function that is normally reserved for the captain. It may be the result of some significant operational failure, or through the discovery of some inappropriate behavior such as the misuse of resources. In these particularly grave instances, the board does have the authority—and the obligation—to temporarily become much more directly engaged in tactical operations until the issue has been resolved.

For example, assume that the captain has been unable to provide appropriate management and bring the budget out of deficit for an extended period of time. The owners (board) might decide, rather than dismissing the captain, to appoint one of the board members to become more actively engaged in helping the captain with analyzing the finances and making a more determined effort to bring the budget into balance. This might involve more day-to-day operational involvement by that individual board member. That board member will be there to help not only resolve the budget issue but also to help the captain become more effective in this key area of management.

Once the budget issue is resolved, that member needs to return to his regular position on the board. Anytime the board is required to cross over into the boundary of management, it should only be with the intent of being a temporary occupying force until the issue is resolved.

Compass Points

✧ Roles and boundaries help the organization work toward common mission success.

✧ Each of the key role-players on the nonprofit ship need to understand their proper relationships with the other key players.

✧ Boundaries are general guidelines but can, under certain circumstances, be crossed over in emergency situations. These exceptions should always be temporary.

Points to Consider

1. How would you describe your organization's key players' (owners, captain, crew, passengers) understanding of their boundaries?

_____

_____

_____

_____

_____

_____

_____

_____

_____

2. Describe an instance in which you think those boundaries may have been inadvertently crossed over. What lessons do you think were learned?

_____
_____
_____
_____
_____
_____
_____

3. What traditional boundary lines between,owners/captain/ crew/passengers might have to be temporarily crossed in your organization in order to resolve an enduring problem?

_____
_____
_____
_____
_____
_____
_____

True Governance

Colby, the executive director of the Central City Arts Foundation, presented his last slide to the board of directors, describing the success of the past quarter. "And so, as you can see, we have met all of our objectives and stayed within budget as promised. Any questions?"

The board sat, eyes glazed over the last twenty minutes, not really realizing that he had finished his presentation. Finally, the board chair, Eustace, voiced an observation.

"I still have a question about the lawn maintenance contract. I think you should have submitted more bids for that contract."

With that, the board seemed to come alive. Several members said they thought that the contract Colby had signed was too generous.

"Sheesh," offered Ralph, "for these conditions, I'd like to have been offered the job."

This comment, and others, led to a thirty-minute conversation about what one should look for in a lawn maintenance contract. Henry, the board chair, was perfectly content with this discussion, even though it was quickly consuming well over 50 percent of the board's remaining time for this quarterly meeting.

Colby tried to explain. "Look, this represents only around 3 percent of the budget, and I did a competitive bid process—"

Eustace interrupted again. "If we don't pay attention to the pennies, then the dollars will disappear. Now, I know something about lawn service. Lord knows, my dearly departed Jake ran a lawn care business for thirty years, and this contract, why it's just giving money away."

The board cheered Eustace on. After all, at the last session, she had brought up the issue of paper clip waste. So many of the board documents that Colby had prepared were held together by these colorful paper clips that she demanded to know why he was using these extravagant paper clips—wasn't this emblematic of his inattention to cost details? It was great watching Eustace in action, a real financial watchdog, not letting Colby get away with anything.

When the meeting had to be drawn to a close, Henry summed up the board's final directives. "Looks like we have consensus on re-bidding the lawn service contract, so, Colby, we'd like you to attend to that. And, let's see, we never got to the part of the agenda about reviewing the strategic alliance offer from New London, nor the agenda item on the new liability insurance, so we'll put that off till the next meeting. Unless there are any objections, I'd like to entertain a motion to adjourn—and see everyone in three months."

CHAPTER 10

CHARTING THE SHIP'S COURSE: STRATEGIC PLANNING

'A ship in port is safe, but that's not what ships are built for.

–Admiral Grace Hopper

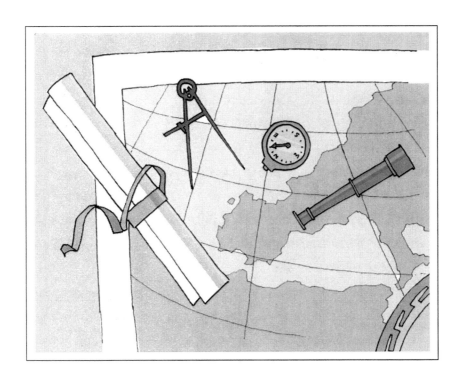

A ship bound for its ultimate destination has to plot its course. Planning for the journey requires research, analysis, and discipline. The planner has to estimate the distance to the destination, the vessel's positional relationship to the final port, the hazards that might lurk within the sea, and the favorable winds or currents that will propel the ship toward its goal. A competent planner considers what strengths and capabilities are required to make this journey. She has to calculate the right amount of fuel and other provisions that must be on board to sustain the trip.

A planner needs a map and other navigational instruments that will reliably indicate the ship's current position relative to its ultimate destination. From that map, a careful estimate of the ship's condition—its internal environment—and the forecasted weather, seas, currents, and perceived obstacles that lie ahead, the ship's leaders can map a journey that determines the best intentional course to take. This requires the right navigational tools, charts, and other instruments that will give the ship's command an accurate depiction of the ship's position at all times, day or night, in good weather or bad.

However, even the best-laid plans, to paraphrase the eighteenth-century poet Robert Burns, often go astray. Then what? Knowing the destination and having a planned route when something forces the vessel off course offers the leadership assurance that the ship, still fully confident of its destination, can make the deliberate path adjustments to recover its course. The destination hasn't changed, but the originally projected pathway has. The ship is forced to make a detour, or course correction, but once it has, it stays true to its promise by re-aiming its bow in the direction of the final port.

But what if there is no strategic plan or direction? Worse, what if there is no map? Then the inclination is to go with the flow of the currents or prevailing winds. If there is no chosen destination, any prevailing wind or current in any direction will seem acceptable. Equally troubling, what happens when dangerous storms arise, or icebergs or reefs come into view? Once again, without any specific, planned direction, the ship's principal strategy is merely to weather the storm or steer around the danger, without any concern about these obstacles affecting the ship's route—*because there is no designated course to which it must return.*

Without a strategy, the ship's leadership plays no active role in shaping the future. Instead it simply becomes a victim of the unfolding, random environment. Have you ever been a member of an organization that felt as if it did nothing but confront one crisis after another, where there was rarely any sense of any forward motion or progress, where the prevalent work was nothing but reacting to sudden fires or seemingly random structural leaks, one after another? These represent classic indicators of an aimless organization, destined never to reach its promised landing because its whole purpose revolves around crisis management. It never redresses the causes of the crises, having long forgotten that the ship has any final destination.

Internal Analysis: The State of the Ship

All planning forces a first discipline of self-assessment that requires looking at both the internal and external environments. For the internal aspect, the planning group must address the aspects of the ship that it can control. The questions should include: How seaworthy is the ship?

Is it structurally sound? Is the ship large enough to hold all the passengers taken aboard, all the way to the envisioned port? Are the sails in good repair and large enough to catch the prevailing winds to propel the ship forward? Does the ship have an alternate means of propulsion (e.g., internal engine) to help move it toward its destination? What if the owners wanted to add more passengers? What will it take to have the right and sufficient resources (people, knowledge, skills, leadership, money, time) to get the ship to that destination successfully?

External Analysis: The Seas, the Weather—Obstacles and Opportunities

No internal analysis can suffice without an interrelated external environmental scan. The strength of the vessel's hull has no significant meaning unless the planning group knows the likely impact of the waves, the probable intensity of storms, and other seaborne threats. On the other hand, strong, favorable winds and currents represent welcome opportunities to move the ship swiftly toward its destination.

The external factors that every nonprofit has to consider in its planning phase represent the external environment that can affect its mission success. The relative health and stability of both national and local economies represent major influences.

The changing needs of the nonprofit's stakeholders will affect what programs to create, enhance, diminish, or eliminate. The changing focus and tastes of donors and what they wish to support are external factors. Foundations and their ever-shifting interests represent key influences.

The political environment, including the development of government funding interests and regulations, can affect an organization's resources dramatically. Technology can greatly enhance or mightily challenge operating procedures and administrative costs.

The external analysis focuses on matters the captain and crew cannot necessarily control but can either try to avoid or even harness to their advantage. They may not be able to alter the stormy seas that lie between the ship and the promised port, but they could become aware enough to navigate the ship into calmer, alternative sea lanes, allowing them to skirt around the tempest. In a wholly different way, the crew cannot generate favorable ocean currents to help move their ship more quickly, but they can know where the favorable currents flow and can navigate so that the ship can slip into those swift-flowing lanes.

Whom to Involve?

Formulating the ship's strategy takes considerable devotion, time, and purposeful effort. Assessing the ship's resources and status, measuring its position and distance relative to the promised destination—or, even more significant, recalling and reminding everyone of where that destination is—and reviewing the forecast for the weather and seas all demand considerable research and a number of diverse perspectives.

The ship's owners (board) have principal responsibility for orchestrating the planning process. This means that the board initiates, oversees, and participates in formulating the strategic direction of the organization. But the board cannot accomplish this successfully without including numerous other views, including those of the captain, crew, passengers, and investors. The owners should also invite the input of experts who know how to predict the seas and weather (economic, political, demographic, and technology specialists). All these views need to be considered and understood so they can be woven into the tapestry of a comprehensive strategic plan which will define the course of the ship over the next several years.

Duration

Thinking strategically has never been more challenging, given the current pace of change in our increasingly interconnected world community. Practically speaking, any such process increases its usefulness by aiming toward a modestly ambitious horizon—most likely a two- to three-year time frame—in which to become fully functional. So the strategic issues focus upon the next several years, predicting how the ship itself might be enhanced and what progress the vessel can make in sailing toward its ultimate destination.

The Strategic Theme

Every two- to three-year strategy bears a significant theme that characterizes it. In the heaving, dangerous seas of the recent Great Recession, many nonprofit vessels created strategies that essentially claimed the theme, "Steady as She Goes," or "Batten Down the Hatches," nautical terms that indicate the vessel will focus on keeping the organization afloat, and not be so concerned with actual progress toward the goal until the seas calm down (i.e., the economy improves). Others may find that their strategies revolve around key accomplishments that must occur within the predicted time, such as "Refitting the Ship" (refurbishing the organization's physical plant or some other tangible aspect of its structure, such as its information technology equipment) or "Replacing the Captain" (notably a concern in the case of the predicted retirement of the long-time executive director and the need to put new leadership in place).

Goals and Objectives

Once the ship's leadership has determined its strategic course of action and direction, the captain and crew take responsibility to forge the tactics and objectives that will form the underlying ways by which those strategies will be accomplished. For example, if the strategic theme is to survive the (economic) storm, some of the underlying goals might be consolidating operations rather than growing, just so the organization can carry on and resume its forward progress after the storm passes. That will include such goals as evaluating the ship's operations (program reviews to look for inefficiencies), lightening the ship's load (eliminating wasteful practices and expenses), or reducing the cargo (adjusting the number of passengers they can serve in the forecasted plan).

Overseeing the Strategy

It will be the responsibility of the board (as the vessel's owners and stewards of the mission) to hold the captain and crew accountable for the successful execution of the strategic plan. This doesn't mean that the owners stand idly by as observers or judge and jury. They, too, have an active responsibility in scanning the horizons, charting the course, encouraging support, and looking for ways to develop resources to help the captain and crew in their endeavors. They may, for example, underwrite the hiring of an organizational development expert to help streamline responsibilities and reduce wasteful overhead costs.

Without a strategy, the ship's leadership plays no active role in shaping the future. Instead it simply becomes a victim of the unfolding, random environment.

Altering the Strategy

In the late nineteenth century, a German general made the keen observation that no battle plan ever survives the first contact with the enemy. In other words, a plan, even a well-considered, strategic one, represents a best guess at the upcoming future and an organization's predicted reaction to it. Circumstances change, despite our best efforts to divine how the future will unfold. No one predicted the great tsunami of 2009. No one foresaw the 9/11 attacks. No one anticipated 2008's Great Recession. As a consequence, the plan has to be adaptive. Such change might not always be bad news. Our ship may encounter a strong, unanticipated wind to its back (for example, an unforeseen bequest from a donor estate) and that could speed up the plan to add a new program or hire that needed part-time crew member. The point is, overall, that the strategy guides the vessel in its every action yet is tempered by the unanticipated events that may arise. Flexibility and adaptability represent key aspects of a sound strategy.

Compass Points

✧ No strategic goals are ever achieved without a purposeful plan.

✧ The board of directors is ultimately responsible for orchestrating and overseeing the strategic planning process.

✧ Effective strategies have a theme.

✧ Strategic plans normally establish goals and objectives for a limited horizon of 2-3 years.

Points to Consider

1. Does your organization have a current strategic plan? If so, how would you describe its theme? What forecasted length of time does it cover?

_____
_____
_____
_____
_____
_____
_____

2. If you don't have a current plan, or the one you last recall expired (e.g., "We're now in year five of our three-year plan"), consider how your organization might benefit from re-initiating a planning process.

_____
_____
_____
_____
_____
_____
_____

3. Consider the critical issue of whose input to the plan would be vital in addressing the strategic issues that confront the organization. Besides the board, executive director, and staff, what other stakeholders should have a voice in this process?

_____
_____
_____
_____
_____
_____
_____

Make It So

Sheila, the newly appointed executive director of People For Puppies, had been reviewing the organization's historic materials during her first three months in this new leadership position. What she found was disconcerting. She knew from her interview process with the board that strategic planning was historically a "sometime thing" with this organization. That is to say, over its twenty-year life there had been stretches of time where the organization lumbered along without any particular strategic direction. What she didn't realize, however, was that even when the organization did place itself under what it considered to be a strategic direction, the plans were quite anemic. Yes, they were professionally assembled in very impressive binders. They contained a number of colorful graphs and charts that purported to demonstrate trends and forecast alternative scenarios that the organization might want to put into operation. There was no evidence within the board's minutes or any other documents that Sheila could find that indicated that the board had ever engaged in continuing oversight of the strategic plan's implementation. It seemed to her as if the planning process represented a brief flurry of activity with no consequential operational impact.

Sheila brought this up with her executive committee, saying that she felt that it was time to create a new strategic plan. The board chair, Dale, agreed that it had been a while since the board had commissioned such a plan.

"Commissioned?" Sheila asked. "Sure," replied Dale, "you know, the staff, they're real good at planning. Why don't you schedule some time to get them together, assemble a plan, and give the board an outline of what they think needs to be done? Then we'll get the board to give it a once-over. And if we've no problems with it, they can go ahead and finalize it into a document that they can use."

Sheila was afraid he would say that. Of course, she had come from a professional for-profit background where planning for the real world was absolutely essential for survival. The old adage, "if you fail to plan, you plan to fail" was part of their corporate wisdom. In her former professional world, the for-profit organization she worked for insisted that the board spearhead the strategic planning process. The board was involved in defining the strategic themes they wanted to see implemented. The staff, while having some input into that process, was tasked with the responsibility of bringing the plan into being by developing support tactics aligned with the strategic themes.

Sheila pressed her point with the executive committee. "I think it's wonderful that you have entrusted the staff with that much involvement in the strategic plan. But I'm concerned that the staff's view, by itself, is a little blinkered."

This comment seemed to anger Oliver, the vice chair. "I have only the highest regard for this staff. They are the champions who have led us to much success in puppy rescue."

Sheila responded, "Listen, I have great confidence in the staff. But their outlook is far from strategic. I have a copy of the latest plan right here. If you look through the major milestones, they all address staff issues. There's plenty in here about staff education, staff recruitment, and other resources the staff feels that it needs to succeed in their assigned programs."

"So?" Dale responded. "These are the people who know what needs to be done. We rely upon their expertise. We're just the board."

Sheila tried to hide her growing exasperation. She had not realized in her interview process how far the board was from understanding its role in strategic planning.

"Dale, let me ask you something. How many admirals in the Navy ask the sailors where to send the fleet?"

Dale looked at her quizzically. "I can't imagine any admiral would do that. What's that got to do with what we're talking about?"

Oliver then interjected, "Oh, I get it. Sheila's trying to tell us that the board of People for Puppies is like admirals in the Navy. We make the big decisions about what the organization does."

Sheila smiled, "Exactly right. The admirals would certainly want to have information about the sailors and what skills the sailors of tomorrow must possess, but their main job is to develop major strategic goals for an entire fleet of ships. The sailors know a lot about their own particular jobs, but not about the fleet."

She opened up the current strategic plan once more. "If you look through this plan," she said, "there are no high-level goals. Nothing in this plan addresses such things as the other organizations in the city who are also trying to promote humane practices toward the dog population and with whom we might form some alliance. There's no comprehensive review of how we might secure new sources of future funding. There's simply an assumption that our past funding will stay essentially the same as in the past three years. Nothing in this plan speaks about developing new ways of educating the public about the importance of our mission. These kinds of high-level goals are not something the program staff will normally think about."

Dale finally began to grasp where Sheila was leading him. "I see your point, but I still don't understand how the board could address these issues, either."

Sheila reassured him, "But that's where the board's greatest value comes in. It should educate itself about the major strategic issues our organization faces. It needs to stay reasonably informed about major trends in dog rescue in general and our community's needs in particular. It should inspire our staff to meet higher challenges and forecast what the organization needs to do to acquire more support over the long haul. Once the board has put the general strategic outline together, then the staff should create the supporting tactics to..."

"Make it so!" interrupted Oliver impetuously. "Just like Jean-Luc Picard would say!"

"Who?" asked Dale.

"You know, the commander on *Star Trek: The Next Generation.* He was always saying that," answered Oliver.

"Oh. Yeah. I was always much more of a Captain Kirk fan, myself," Dale responded.

CHAPTER 11

THE INVESTORS: THE DONORS

"Pray to God, but keep rowing to shore."

—*Russian Proverb*

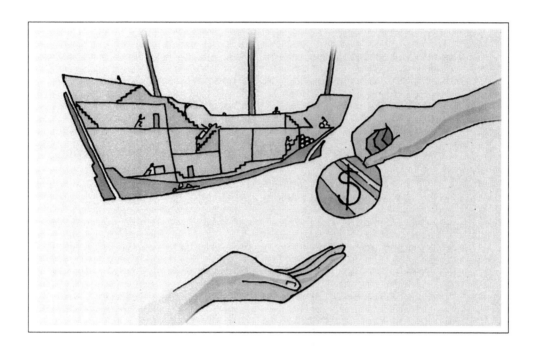

Building and maintaining the ship requires capital investment. While the nobility of the nonprofit ship's values and vision provides the psychic energy and goodwill, none of that will count unless it is finally transformed into cold, hard cash. The stark but practical mantra, "No money, no mission" should remain ever present on the lips of the ship's founders, owners, captain, and crew.

The nautical metaphor discussed in this chapter represents an ideal new way of reframing nonprofit efforts to bring in vital funds. This model demands striking the term *fundraising* from our vocabulary. Ships require investors. The ships that transported Columbus to discover the New World, as well as the thousands of ships that brought settlers from Europe to colonize it, were not built by bake sales and walk-a-thons. Monarchs and the merchant class formed corporations, attracted investors' money, promised them a handsome return on their investment. This money fueled the shipbuilding and hiring of crews, the enlistment of passengers and fortune seekers to take the journey over the Atlantic. Of course, many of those passengers had other reasons for boarding the ships. Some looked for religious and political freedom; others sought adventure in a New World. But none of them could have made the journey without the investors' critical participation in creating the fleets that would transport them.

Using this same reframing and renaming (from *fundraising* to *investment*) has overwhelming appeal to an evolving class of donors. These are the people and institutions that have abandoned the traditional forms of giving simply for giving's sake. The old, dying model of philanthropic appeal rested on the fundamental belief, for example, that the "poor will always be with you." In that framed way of thinking, poverty (as well as any other number of social ills), were regarded as endless conditions. Donors were asked to give, but with no expectations beyond the entrenched belief that one should always give to that unrelenting and unsolvable condition.

The evolving class of nonprofit supporters looks upon their money as a tool to resolve the underlying cause of the condition. They don't want simply to give their money to the poor. Many have become convinced that the old form of handing out money works as an enablement, only prolonging the suffering. They want their money to eliminate the conditions that lead to, and condemn people to remain in, poverty's relentless cycle. Those investors not only want to help shelter a homeless family on a particular night, they want their money to help the homeless find a way out of the homelessness labyrinth.

This new investor class brings a new language to the nonprofit realm, using terms such as *return on investment, operational efficiencies*, and *business plans*. They may even demand a prospectus, an explanation of the business plan that any prudent investor would want to review before deciding whether to invest. These investors also will want proven assurance that the enterprise is well-governed by a resolute, dedicated board and managed by competent professionals.

All of this fits well into the nautical metaphor. Using the concept of the nonprofit ship as the vehicle to transport, for example, people who suffer from drug addiction to a new shore where they have been freed from their addiction speaks to the very essence of this investor mind-set. The power of demonstrating that the requested funds will have a transformative effect—changing lives, changing communities, changing the world— resonates deeply with potential investors.

The nonprofit-as-ship has another powerful advantage in its persuasive imagery and language. The new age of philanthropic investors, especially the institutional ones such as grant-making foundations, prefer to invest their money in specific programs or activities that help lead to very tangible results or outcomes. They shy away from funding routine expenses that are necessary to keep the enterprise running but lack any dramatic, immediate payback. So when a nonprofit makes an appeal for specific improvements, for example in its computer hardware or software resources, it becomes a real challenge to excite investors.

The phrase that has been used almost to exhaustion in the nonprofit sector for this specific kind of help is "capacity building." While it does offer a hint of what the funding will be used to accomplish—everything from increased physical space to the less tangible things like enhancing staff skills—the phrase has a sleep-inducing, abstract vagueness about it. By expressing the need using the more vivid, metaphorical ship language, an investor may be more readily convinced.

To gain investor support, the applicant has to connect the nautical dots by using more resourceful imagery. She will emphasize that use of the money to improve some part of the nonprofit's operation is similar to enlarging part of the ship, or re-engineering the ship's hull so it will slice through the waves more efficiently, increasing its speed, thus hastening the delivery of the ship's passengers to that envisioned shore.

Transforming the terminology from *donors* to *investors* also implies building a long-term relationship. A donation will be seen and experienced as a simple, one-time transaction. A donor tosses a quarter into the offering box under the presumption that somehow, somewhere it will accomplish some good. An investor, though, puts money into the enterprise with a deeper anticipation of later following the good effect that it had. Investors want to stay tuned in, want to witness the growth of their investment.

This relationship can blossom and bloom over long expanses of time. The long-term investors will recall being present when the nonprofit craft was not much bigger than a rowboat, now that it has grown into a stately square-rigger. They will have witnessed its early history when the small rowboat could deliver only a few passengers to their promised destination, and only after enormous effort and time. Now they witness the three-masted tall ship delivering thousands to that shore. Most important, they will recognize that it was their faithful, continuous investments that allowed the ship to expand and bring about this wider, more successful impact.

The ship's owners (board) need to see themselves as investors, too. Obviously, they have signed on to invest their valued time and skills in overseeing the ship's successful operation. As part of rounding out that role, the board should enact a policy committing each director to making a personal, annual monetary investment as well. While the board may not want to set an expectation of certain amount, the critical factor centers on the concept that all will give something, so the board can say with proud assurance that 100 percent of the board invests more than just its time, but its money as well, to assure the ship's success.

That assurance represents a key factor in the next dimension of the board's role in investment—that of convincing others to become investors in the organization. Many people accept the position of nonprofit board member and make the automatic assumption that somehow this absolves them of any role in helping to bring in money. They will assume that fund development is a task for the staff, or for hired experts in the arcane arts of grant writing or orchestrating fundraising events. Those kinds of board members wistfully imagine that they may have a role in observing and commenting on fund development, but won't be called upon to deal with the unsavory aspects of actually doing it. Once again, the reframing of this term—away from *fundraising*, which normally makes most board members flinch in pain—to one that sounds and actually is more inviting—*investment*—can make all the difference in helping the board members to participate in this way.

Here's the underlying, logical appeal of reframing *fundraising* to *investing* for a board member. As described in chapter 6, board members are the legal and moral owners of the nonprofit ship on behalf of all those who are served by the mission. Consider how the owners of a for-profit are always looking for investors to put up the necessary capital to help grow the enterprise, all in exchange for a share in the ownership of the company. In the nonprofit case, however, the board members, as moral owners, are out asking investors for the capital to grow the nonprofit's operational success and in exchange, those investors are being offered, not a share in the organization's actual ownership, but credit for helping the mission advance. Those investors should be promised a return on their investment—not as money in their pockets, but as real, substantive change in the community and in the hunger eliminated, the violence eradicated, the disease conquered. Those represent incalculable returns on investment.

Even with the advantage of relabeling and re-thinking the activity from fundraising to investment procurement, many nonprofit ship owners will still need help in understanding ways to attract investors. A significant part of this help comes from assembling materials that explain how the money will be invested, much like a for-profit develops a prospectus. In the nonprofit world, this is called a case statement. It explains precisely how the money will be invested within the organization to bring about the promised effect on those being served, why now represents the right time to invest, and why the intended investor is an ideal participant. This basic document equips the board members with the fundamental, persuasive logic they need to influence investors.

Despite all the supporting literature, training, encouragement, and support, some board members will still be unwilling to take on such an active, direct role in procuring investors. The board then needs to find even more inventive ways to engage those individuals in the investor quest. A strong alternative role might be for those board members to simply be the door-openers, the ones who will set up the meetings with their personal contacts so the investment pitch can be made by another board member to that prospective investor. Another, similar approach would be to ask a reluctant board member to accompany the asking board member—to lend a personal endorsement without the burden of actually asking for the investment. The point is, the board should find ways in which every board member (owner) plays a significant role in the endless quest for investments to keep the ship strong, growing in capacity, and sailing assuredly toward delivering its passengers to the envisioned destination.

Compass Points

✧ No money, no mission.

✧ Reframe the concepts of donations and fundraising into investments toward mission success.

✧ Investment invites long-term commitment compared to the term donation.

✧ The board (ship owners) has a deep obligation in the quest to find and grow investors.

Points to Consider

1. In what ways does your organization attract people to contribute to it?

_____

_____

_____

_____

_____

_____

_____

152

2. If you were to think of your donors more as investors, in what ways would this change your methods and approach to asking for their support?

_____

_____

_____

_____

_____

_____

_____

3. To what extent is your board "invested" in helping via their own contributions? What percent of your board contributes to your organization annually? How might you increase that number to 100 percent?

_____

_____

_____

_____

_____

_____

_____

4. How would you describe your board's involvement in asking potential investors for funding? How might you increase its participation rate in bringing in resources?

_____

_____

_____

_____

_____

_____

_____

Building the Investment Group

The 80/20 rule—the observation that 80 percent of the work gets accomplished by 20 percent of the people assigned to it—was in full force and about to destroy the board of directors at the Living Community Gardens (LCG). Woodrow, the board chair, tried to reign in the heated exchange which he feared would erupt, but the full force of the argument was still building.

Deidre was beside herself with anger after Rand made the comment that the board's resource committee was not meeting its goals. "No, Rand, you've completely missed the point. This committee—just the five of us—has just, by ourselves, brought in close to 80 percent of what the board had apportioned to it in terms of outside donations. The rest of you—fifteen people—have not done a single thing to help us get to that number."

Rand just offered a smirking reply, "But Deidre, that's your job—you're the development committee. You guys are the ones who said you'd raise the funds. The rest of us aren't any good at this kind of work. That's why we created your group. And I just was remarking that it was a shame that you've fallen short, by, well, 20 percent."

Deidre's eyes widened with intensity, "No, no, no, Rand. You have forgotten what our committee charter states," she asserted as she pulled

Ships require investors. The ships that transported Columbus to discover the New World, as well as the thousands of ships that brought settlers from Europe to colonize it, were not built by bake sales and walk-a-thons. Transforming the terminology from donors to investors also implies building a long-term relationship.

out the document. "The Development Committee will lead and support the board's efforts in raising the necessary funds as outlined in the Living Community Gardens' annual budget. That's clearly stating that the full board has to be engaged in fundraising."

The other board members, the ones who were not on Deidre's development committee and had, like Rand, been content with cheering her on while finding ways to "miss" her email or voicemail calls for help, sat silently, hoping Rand would not infuriate her more, lest she start casting her resentment at the rest of them, too.

Rand acknowledged Deidre's point, but still maintained that since she and the other committee members had some form of background and experience in this fund-development area, it was really best to leave such things to them.

"No use trying to teach us old dogs any new tricks," Rand commented with that smirk again, looking for approving nods from his fellow reluctant fund developers.

Deidre, deciding to press the point in a different way, responded, "OK, Rand, I want to know what the "old dogs" are going to do if my committee members just resign from that responsibility. You know, we're finished being the only ones who help in this way. We're burned out, done."

Woodrow felt it necessary to step in at this point. As board chair, he couldn't simply preside over the board's self-destruction.

"Okay, okay, I believe we all get the picture here. Two years ago we all agreed that, to meet LCG's strategic goals, the board had to become more active in fund development. We re-activated the development committee after years of dormancy, and Deidre and her people have done a great job of getting it underway. But maybe we're experiencing the effects of them being too successful. They have accomplished a lot despite the reluctance shown by the rest of us to join with them."

Alicia, the board's secretary, then offered her perspective. "I had a similar experience with a board I served with several years ago, and they overcame this problem by coming up with a creative list of various ways of involving the board in bringing in money.

"The first thing we did," she explained, "was to establish a set amount of dollars that the board was responsible for bringing in. Then—and here's where we became creative—we brainstormed various ways each board member could bring in money. The first, most obvious way is to commit to asking for money, the traditional way of soliciting money. But then, we collectively came up with other ways we could participate."

"Such as…?" pressed Rand.

"A lot of them were really unorthodox, but they worked. For example, we allowed a board member to fulfill her quota by finding ways to offset expenses. Julie, a board member who works at an office supply store, was able to secure a huge in-kind donation of paper, something like $2500 worth, and the board said that qualified as meeting her obligation—it was the same as if she had asked for and received a $2500 donation."

"Then we got even more inventive," Alicia pressed on. "Two of our board agreed to go to the State House and testify before a legislative committee on behalf of the people we were helping, those with this rare disease, so that funding wouldn't be cut. They saved our agency from losing almost $10,000 that year. The board counted that rescue of funding as the moral equivalent of raising $10,000."

At this point, even Rand was becoming interested in hearing more. "What else?" he asked.

"Oh, plenty," Alicia continued. "Let's see, we had some people fulfill their obligation by providing their time—lots of hours of set-up and tear-down for our annual gala—and others, like Estelle, well, you know, she runs that second-hand store. She's a superb negotiator, and our executive director got her to use those skills to get our best deal on contract work to refurbish the administrative office. Saved at least $7500 off the original estimate. And, yes, that counted—just as if she had gone out and brought back a check written out for that amount."

The board's mood had brightened at this set of examples. "The big point is," Alicia emphasized, "to get a very comprehensive list of ways members can fulfill our commitment in their own, individual ways, and then make sure everyone literally signs up for his or her chosen method. Then we all have a chance to do the things we enjoy or are best at, and, most important, we all, in our unique ways, bring in resources."

"I'm sure you have some slackers," Deidre commented briefly, darting her eyes at Rand.

Alicia was prepared for that observation. "Sure, some people, for whatever reason, are not able to do anything. We did have an "escape clause" for our board. We said if you cannot or will not choose from our long list of options, then you must make a significant, personal gift of money. It offered people who may be extremely busy another option to show solidarity with the rest of the board."

As the conversation continued, the board ultimately agreed to have the development committee draft a similar list of optional ways to bring in money. For the first time in memory, they stood at the threshold of resolving this heated issue in a truly productive manner.

CHAPTER 12

LIFEBOATS AND LIFE PRESERVERS: RISK AND RESPONSE

'The sea finds out everything you did wrong.

–Francis Stokes

W hen the *Titanic* sank on that frigid April night in 1912, only 711 of the 2,201 passengers and crew survived. Almost 70 percent of those on board perished. Unable to secure a place in a lifeboat, most died quickly, freezing to death in the 28-degree North Atlantic waters. Even given adequate time to rescue everyone, at best the ship had only enough lifeboats to save 1,178 persons, roughly 50 percent of those on board. Despite that alarming fact, the ship was in compliance with British regulations, since the law in 1912 based the number of required lifeboats upon the tonnage of the ship, not the number of passengers.[4]

Reeling from the horror of this loss of life, the international community soon adopted a policy that required all passenger ships to carry an adequate number of lifeboats in order to save everyone on board.

This historic example of failed maritime risk management still echoes a century later. The image of any loss of life from a ship's sinking always leads to outcries questioning whether the ship's preparedness for saving lives was fully thought out. The nonprofit ship's owners have to reflect on how they want to responsibly address the various risks their nonprofit ship must confront.

Risk is an undesired event which may or may not occur. Life in general, and sea voyages in particular, encounter innumerable risks. Navigating through them requires sound judgment in assessing their potential impact and probability, then deciding on the appropriate action.

---

[4] Mersey and Gough-Calthorpe, *Loss of the Steamship "Titanic,"* 56, 67.

Risks have to be considered for their eventual likelihood and their potential impact. The process starts with assessing the probability that the risk will actually take place. For example, one might estimate that a ship of a certain size, with a certain experienced crew, taking a known route with a set of particular hazards has a one in one hundred chance of not reaching its destination.

The next step is to assign a cost to that loss. Thinking purely in terms of the monetary value of the ship and its cargo can be relatively easy. But other losses, including the more intangible ones such as lives, health, reputation, or public trust, can be equally devastating to the ship's ability to continue as an enterprise. These risks elude the easy assignment of a dollar figure.

Once a risk is identified and assessed in terms of its potential damage, the next step is to find ways to address the risk. The first option is to ignore it. This choice may come about because its consequences are considered too negligible or, at the other end of the spectrum, too inescapably large, to do anything to avoid or diminish them. For example, the ship's owners could take up the issue of how to address the possibility of the ship encountering the sudden eruption of a tsunami that comes barreling at the vessel at 200 miles per hour. Depending on the ship's position, there may be no way to avoid this random act of nature. The only reasonable alternative for this risk is to hope it never occurs. This would be the equivalent of a nonprofit board considering what to do if the city were to be struck by a football stadium–sized meteor. Let's not worry about contingency plans for that one, since it would likely evaporate most of the hemisphere.

The next alternative in addressing a risk is to look for ways to avoid it altogether. Within the ship metaphor, that could mean never allowing the ship to lose sight of the shore. This will certainly keep the ship safer, keeping it away from the deep water hazards, but there are still other dangers such as rocks and reefs that can tear up a ship sailing close to a shoreline. Even more worrisome is the very real likelihood that if the ship never leaves the sight of the shore—or, to be absolutely safe, not even the harbor—its passengers will never get to the promised destination. An analogously risk-avoiding nonprofit would likely take a very long time to make any impact on the people it intends to serve. Its timidity will always smother its creativity; its fear of failure will act as a continuous brake on producing any meaningful results.

The third alternative represents a much bolder response to risk. In this case, the answer to risk is, "Weaken it." Thus, in the case of a ship that's concerned about passengers being able to survive the rough seas, the risk response is to strengthen the whole ship so that it won't break apart in those rough seas or, as an alternative, to add lifeboats to the ship so that the passengers have a fighting chance of surviving and being rescued should the ship go down. Notice in this case how dramatically different the results are compared to avoiding the risk. Rather than hugging the shore, the ship forges boldly toward its vision, well into deep water but with proper fortifications or equipped with alternatives. In a nonprofit, this principle might play out like this: The board decides to deploy a new program to test its effectiveness. At the same time, it puts a trial contingency plan in place that allows the new program to be altered or discontinued should the expected outcomes not materialize.

The final alternative in confronting risk can be expressed in one phrase: spread it. In this approach, the ship looks for a partner to help take on responsibility for the risk. This is most clearly manifested in insurance agreements. In the ship metaphor, this approach would involve looking to an insurer to help with the payment for damage to the ship or loss of cargo. In a larger application of this approach, however, the ship might actually partner with another ship, one that had a stronger, more capable, proven ability to overcome seaborne dangers, and ask that ship to take the passengers through dangerous waters.

In the nonprofit world, this example manifests itself through various forms of insurance coverage the owners purchase to protect different components of the ship. This includes directors' and officers' insurance to protect the owners and crew managers from the costs associated with lawsuits; property insurance to protect against potential losses for damage to the physical premises and equipment; liability insurance to protect against the losses that might occur from crew or passenger injuries; and fidelity insurance against embezzlement.

The primary need for risk management in the arena of financial sustainability begins with looking at the sources the nonprofit relies upon for its revenue. Understanding how money comes into the organization through various means such as grants, individual donors, third-party contracts, earned revenue, special fundraising events, and endowments is the first step in identifying potential risk. If a nonprofit finds that it has an over-reliance on one or two sources that bring in most of its revenue, that should be a cause for concern. If one of those major sources were to suddenly disappear, how would the organization survive financially? In this instance, the risk management choice should be to weaken the threat through diversifying revenue streams through as many potential methods as possible.

Life in general and sea voyages in particular, encounter innumerable risks. Navigating through them requires sound judgment in assessing their potential impact and probability, then deciding on the appropriate action.

If the organization enjoys the blessings of significant financial reserves or endowments, those, too, qualify for some form of risk management. The owners should create a policy that guides the investment strategy for those funds, assuring responsible financial return while also being cautious about avoiding highly volatile investment choices.

The nonprofit also faces the risk of its finances being stolen or embezzled. Aside from considering insurance, in order to share the risk, a more effective response might be to weaken the risk itself. This can be accomplished through instituting proper accounting controls and procedures that will minimize this chance of avoidable loss.

The ship's owners must also confront the risks that the passengers face. Many nonprofits serve people who are particularly vulnerable. Children, others who are physically or mentally challenged, and the elderly need special consideration in protecting them from harm. Once again, the answer to this risk is to weaken it to the point of near-impossibility by insisting, for example, on background checks for anyone that the ship decides to bring on board as crew.

There are other areas of risk that should be considered as part of responsible risk management. These typically fall under an operational category. A ship will oftentimes make sure that it isn't disabled at sea by having an inventory of spare parts on board. A nonprofit will ensure that its operational capability is not easily hobbled by a sudden, unexpected loss of equipment or services by creating a proper disaster recovery plan. For example, a nonprofit hospital would be exercising sound operational risk management by ensuring that it has a robust ability to generate its own power for a limited amount of time in the event of a major power outage. Other common areas to protect are information databases or other critical information technology software and hardware.

Compass Points

✧ Risk management means identifying what the risks are and what the appropriate response should be to each risk.

✧ Risk management allows four possible responses:

    1. Live with it

    2. Avoid it

    3. Weaken it

    4. Share it

✧ Risk management should focus on financial protection, stakeholder safety, and operational issues.

Points to Consider

1. What do you see as the areas of primary risk that your organization addresses?

_____

_____

_____

_____

_____

_____

_____

2. Among the four possible alternatives discussed in risk management, which do you feel your organization uses the most? How effective do you feel the primary selection is in managing risk?

_____

_____

_____

_____

_____

_____

_____

3. What forms of insurance does your nonprofit have in place to protect the owners, passengers, and crew? What procedure does the board use for reviewing these protective policies to insure they cover your risks appropriately?

_____
_____
_____
_____
_____
_____
_____

Eggs in One Basket

The first power spike caused the office lights to flutter momentarily, then dim, followed by a darkened silence. Every workstation at the High Hopes Adult Literacy center abruptly shut down simultaneously. Within moments, the power sprang back into action, the lights flashed back on, and the HVAC systems grumbled back to life. The staff powered up their work stations as the hard drives spun into restoral mode. Everything seemed to be working until the staff tried to log back into the database systems on the network server.

"Looks like the server has still not rebooted," muttered Renée, as she tried to recover her report. Twenty minutes later, with the server still not responding, the High Hopes office manager called their tech support contractor to come out to run some diagnostics.

Within the hour, the tech programmer had arrived. Peering into the machinery beneath the cover, he made his grim assessment. "Dude, she is totally fried. There's not a circuit board inside that hasn't been completely toasted. Hard drive is completely seized up, too. Never going to see that data again. Looks like the cage chassis is still usable, so you got that going for you."

Liza, the executive director, clearly didn't need this news, especially today, as the staff was preparing reports for tomorrow's board meeting. "How soon can you get us restored with new parts?"

"I'm not sure," the tech guy replied. "Probably within the next day or so. If you have our Gold Plan coverage, you know, the one that puts your emergency at the top of our priority list, we could have it done by tomorrow around noon."

Liza's stomach went into its third knot at this remark. "Gold Plan," she thought. "We didn't feel we could justify that kind of cost when we renewed the maintenance plan. We couldn't even afford the 'Zinc Plan,' had there even been that option."

"We just opted for the regular monthly maintenance plan," she explained, "so what does that mean?"

The tech looked at his worksheet. "Wow—that puts you all to an estimated restoral time of early next week. We have at least twelve other groups who have higher-paid priority coverage and we have to get to them first. Bummer."

Liza then returned to an earlier comment the technician had made about the hard drive. "You said something about the hard drive earlier— what did you mean?"

The technician held the small, metallic, oblong box in the palm of his hand.

"This was where all your common files were held. The power spike pretty well cooked it. If you have your recovery files saved on a back-up drive, this is no big deal."

"Back-up drive?" Liza thought. "What's a back-up drive?"

Liza felt lightheaded and weak as her mind began to spin though potential options to keep the nonprofit functional over the next week—all the email, web access, reports, and, my God, what about the big Webinar we're scheduled to deliver to a hundred participants on Friday? With her whole information technology hub a darkened ruin, there would be no access to the Web, all her staff's productivity would drop to zero, and none of her programs for her online literacy courses would be working.

She strained her wits looking for potential alternatives but with no previous recovery planning, Liza's brain was trapped in a panicked loop, unable to fathom how she would handle this evolving calamity.

CHAPTER 13

BEACONS AND SIGNALS: BROADCASTING THE SHIP'S PRESENCE

Ships that pass in the night, and speak each other in passing,
Only a signal shown and a distant voice in the darkness;
So on the ocean of life we pass and speak one another…

–Henry Wadsworth Longfellow

O ne of the most heartbreaking moments in the recounting of the *Titanic's* sinking occurs when the ship, its hull ripped apart by the iceberg, lists gravely in the water as a crewmember fires a distress flare into the cold, moonless, night sky. The flares ascends, bursts briefly, illuminating the unfolding tragedy below, and then extinguishes itself as it floats into the freezing ocean water. Unknown to those desperately hoping for rescue, the flares were sighted by watchmen on the SS *Californian* a few miles away. Those crewmen did not interpret the signals as signs of distress. Just before then, the *Californian's* radio specialist had grown tired, shut down the radio receiver, and gone to bed. The *Titanic's* radio distress calls went unheard by the one ship that was near enough to have rescued the passengers.

This failed attempt to communicate to a nearby ship to come to the *Titanic's* aid is emblematic of many nonprofit "ships" that attempt to send signals for public support. Those signals may or may not be strong enough to reach their intended contacts. Or the messages themselves may be misunderstood or ignored. In fact, if a nonprofit fails repeatedly in its attempts to promote its presence, its good intentions, and its need for financial and other resource support, it, too, could experience the same fate as the *Titanic*.

In the long history of seafaring, ships have used varying methods of communicating their presence, indicating under whose jurisdiction they sail, signaling their intentions to other vessels, or demonstrating they are in trouble and need assistance. The Greeks used various signaling flags, a tradition that has evolved into an international standard today. Beyond these kinds of symbols, seagoing vessels had to resort to sounds such fog horns, whistles, or lights when lack of visibility was an issue. These signaling systems became much more sophisticated in the modern age with the introduction of radio signals. Still, no matter which method or how old, the use of a clear set of agreed-upon, understandable signals became absolutely essential for successful seaborne travel.

Marketing to the Passengers

A ship's ability to communicate with its various potential audiences is absolutely vital. In the competitive shipping industry, commercial ships must advertise their services to attract the cargo and passengers they wish to convey. In the very same way, a nonprofit cannot hope to succeed if it cannot know what its passengers want—the destination they require— and, once that is clear, proceed with two major tasks: (1) prepare to sail toward that destination; and (2) inform the passengers how, when, and where to board.

Staying in contact with those whom the nonprofit serves represents a primal obligation. Everything the nonprofit wants to accomplish in its quest for mission success must ultimately be a reflection of the needs of those it serves. To misunderstand that, to not stay current with passenger needs as they evolve, frustrates any mission success.

For example, if a nonprofit proclaims its mission is to champion historic preservation in a community, it will never be able to successfully enlist anyone to come along on its journey if it has only a sketchy understanding of the whole scope of potential properties that it might want to include, or fails to appreciate how each of those properties should be restored in order to preserve its authentic artistic and architectural integrity.

The only way to avoid this disaster comes through the organization's immersion into grasping the issues that define the stakeholders' needs. Through research involving surveys, focus groups, or any means of opening a constant communication channel with those to be served, the nonprofit can begin to shape, mold, and adapt its activities to fit those contours and then map the course.

The second crucial component in marketing to the stakeholders revolves around issuing the word to all who need to know: this ship is here, ready to take you to this well-defined, ideal destination—and here's how to find us. Both the message and the medium used to get the message into the heads and hearts of the potential passengers present critical considerations. Reflect, for example, upon a nonprofit that wants to serve those who suffer from some rare illness, one that is relatively obscure, but devastating nonetheless. This organization wants to offer support to those diagnosed with this disease and to their families. It promises to develop support groups, influence more physicians who specialize in the treatment of this disease to move into the community, and advocate for more government funding to research the disease's cause and eventual cure. How can that fledgling nonprofit get the word out to its potential population?

One very effective way will be by word of mouth. Using the network of those who created this nonprofit—presumably a number of persons who are contending with this malady directly or indirectly—is a solid first step. Next, the organization must focus on connecting with the medical community. This will include engaging with hospitals, clinics, and physicians, informing them about this new group, and putting literature and reference materials into their hands so they can let those contending with the disease know where they can find support.

This, of course, carries the obligation of making the nonprofit organization easy to contact. This once meant having a physical mailing address, a phone that could be answered, and perhaps some actual office space. Nowadays, a virtual presence is mandatory—establishing a website, being accessible via email, and using various social media such as Facebook, Twitter, LinkedIn, and YouTube to maximize the organization's public visibility and "reach-ability."

Marketing to the Investors

The nonprofit ship must also attract contributors (see investors, Chapter 11) whose funding is essential to maintain, expand, or otherwise enhance the ship's seafaring capabilities. The message has to be tailored for that distinct audience; it must be substantially different than the communication strategy for the ship's potential passengers.

Consider this particular example: a small nonprofit in a large Midwestern city began its existence on the fundamental premise that no child in that city should ever suffer from hunger. The founders used this basic belief to attract a governing board, volunteers, and donors so they could build a series of programs to eradicate that form of suffering among children in their community. They proclaim a simple belief: relieving hunger is a community responsibility and, as a part of that community, we are pledged to do all we can to bring about a new future where no child has to endure malnutrition. They encapsulate that message in all of their communications.

That astonishingly bold proclamation, broadcasted into the community, has two principal audiences: families who have hungry children and those who share the belief that help should be given to hungry children. For the first group, this message is a call to "come aboard" this ship, because its mission is to deliver the children from hunger. Equally important, but to a wholly different audience, is the clear call to support—through donations and service—this ship and its voyage.

To succeed, a nonprofit must enlist and surround itself with people who believe what it believes to be good and right and true. The core of any nonprofit's message to the community answers the essential question of *why* it exists. It must state what public good it wishes to bring about, either eliminating some unwanted community condition (e.g., hunger, illness, poverty, violence, ignorance) or promoting some beneficial community attribute (e.g., more public art, more parks).

Answering the "Why" question, as Simon Sinek explains in his book *Start with Why*[5], appeals to people at their emotional core. The answer to "Why?" does not seek to find resolution in the logical part of our minds—in fact, many nonprofit answers to the Why question may seem fantastically irrational. Cure cancer? Save the planet? Eliminate heart disease? End war?

Any nonprofit wanting to enlist support sends out this beacon, or signal, looking to awaken and engage those who are tuned into that particular, heartfelt frequency. Those people are out there, ready to receive. The marketing effort focuses on those whose dials are already set to that

---

[5] Sinek, *Start with Why.*

frequency, not on convincing others to switch their dials to that frequency.

We can draw two very important conclusions from these thoughts. First, no one will respond unless the nonprofit ship transmits its resonating signal to the world—that clear and distinguishable harmonic tone proclaiming what it believes in, the essential Why of its existence. That signal will vibrate in those whose hearts are already prepared to respond. Secondly, for those who are not attuned to that harmonic frequency, well, don't trouble yourselves over them. As one perceptive nonprofit marketing expert once offered, "If your mission is to rescue puppies, then those who love dogs are going to respond. But don't waste your time trying to convert the cat people."

Once a nonprofit has made clear the Why of its organization and by that process gained the attention of those inclined to invest time and money, the next critical step is answering the What question. If the Why question targeted the public's heart, then the What question informs and reassures the rational side of the brain that the ship's operational approach in responding to the targeted need will produce results. The answer to the What question has to demonstrate that the organization's approach to resolving the problem is based on sound reason and competent business strategies.

In the example of the nonprofit trying to end child hunger in a community, the organization would point to the programs it employs to get food to the children as well as other actions that help break the cycle that has led to this abiding problem in the first place. The organization would point out how inventive and successful it has become in putting sound operating practices into place. It would confidently prove how the overwhelming majority of each donated dollar is being converted into food, not going up the chimney in administrative overhead expense. It would demonstrate its unmistakably clear outcomes showing how child hunger is disappearing, anchored in solid, rigorous research methodology.

In the long history of seafaring, ships have used varying methods of communicating their presence, indicating under whose jurisdiction they sail, signaling their intentions to other vessels, or demonstrating they are in trouble and need assistance. The message is critical to proclaim, but there's an equally important factor: one must also consider the different ways in which the message can be sent out.

The message is critical to proclaim, but there's an equally important factor: one must also consider the different ways in which the message can be sent out. This decision revolves around identifying the best ways to communicate with those whom the nonprofit wants to reach with its message. Just as ships must choose among the use of flags, lights, flares, and radio to signal for support, a nonprofit must consider what forms of media it should use to beckon others to join in its mission efforts. Which form is most likely to be seen and heard by the prospective investors? If a group selects a method that no one is likely to see, feel, or hear, its organization will be replicating that same pointless act of the dying *Titanic*—shooting a lonely flare into the night sky, too distant or obscure to be seen or interpreted by anyone who might be inclined to help.

Among the various media available as delivery systems are traditional print, radio, and television. In the past decade, there's been a sea change in terms of alternate web-based media that also offer a rich set of means to broadcast your message to the waiting public. That recent transformation made available by social media has offered nonprofits as big a leap in communication as the seaborne vessels witnessed with the introduction of radios. Think of it: for thousands of years, seagoing vessels could communicate only as far as the eye could see or ear could hear. Once radio was brought into the equation, the reach of a ship's communication capabilities took a quantum leap.

The Messengers

Fully staffed seagoing vessels will normally have signalmen on board in charge of communicating the ship's position, status, or other vital information with the rest of the world. Some nonprofits will have the blessing of a staff person with that expertise on board the ship. That individual will have the responsibility for the content of the marketing message and will oftentimes have the expertise necessary to employ the various web-based media, such as updating the website or posting news on Facebook. For small nonprofits with less robust crew capabilities, this function will default to the executive director (captain) or, in many cases, to the board of directors (owners).

No matter what capabilities may be present in the crew, the board, representing the ownership of the ship, has a substantial role to play in the ship's communication activity. The owners have the exclusive power to modify the mission, based on the changing needs of those the mission serves. It is therefore imperative that the owners stay involved in understanding those ever-evolving requirements. A second and equally critical responsibility is the board's role in evangelizing the ship's "good news" to the community at large.

The ship's owners are required to play an active role in promoting the ship's vision and mission—the Why and the What messages—in order to attract funding (see investors, chapter 11) and continuously bolster the ship's image in the eyes of the public. To accomplish this, owners have to develop a toolkit of useful methods to formulate and deliver the message. These tools will include items such as the "elevator speech," a quick, conversational guide that explains in a few moments the ship's purpose, to more formal items such as a prepared, twenty-minute PowerPoint presentation that can be easily used by board members who are willing to make a public appeal in a community forum.

Compass Points

⟡ A nonprofit needs to formulate its core message to deliver to two distinct audiences: the passengers it wants to invite on the journey, and those they are asking to help support this mission. The answer to the "Why We Exist" question is based on values and speaks to people's hearts.

⟡ The answer to the "What We Do" question addresses operational matters and reassures the logical side of the brain's need for things to make sense.

⟡ Sending the message in the proper medium is critical as well—selecting the appropriate method most likely to reach the proper audience.

⟡ No matter what expertise the crew may have in marketing, the board must play a dynamic role in broadcasting the ship's good news.

Points to Consider

1. How does your organization currently make itself known to those it intends to serve (its potential passengers)? How effective is that approach?

_____

_____

_____

_____

_____

_____

_____

2. How would your organization currently answer the key question of Why We Exist?

_____

_____

_____

_____

_____

_____

_____

3. How should your organization respond to the question of What We Do to assure both those you serve and those who support you that you're successful?

_____
_____
_____
_____
_____
_____
_____

4. Describe who has primary responsibility for the ship's messaging to passengers and investors. What role does the board currently play? How might it be enhanced?

_____
_____
_____
_____
_____
_____
_____

Signal Loss

"I am delighted to report," began Arnold, the board chair of St Swithin's Outreach Center, "that we are moving closer and closer to mission success. The number of homeless families that need our services shows a continuing decline for the third straight quarter. My friends, at this rate, we might very well have solved the problem of homelessness in this part of our city by late next year!"

The rest of the board beamed at this welcome news. It seemed unusual that in the midst of the region's economic downturn and glacially slow recovery, success could be so near.

The executive director, Eva, was not nearly as enthused as Arnold. She and Arnold were continually at odds over interpreting the statistics. Because of declining donations over the past three years, Eva was forced to let her part-time outreach coordinator go. This loss had cut St Swithin's major communication channel to government agencies that coordinated homeless policies throughout the region. St. Swithin's voice was now rarely heard in the occasional homelessness roundtables sponsored by several neighborhood community ministries.

Eva spoke up to quell the rising enthusiasm. "I am concerned that although we've seen a decline in our numbers, the homeless problem still persists in this city and, in fact, may getting more severe." Arnold was displeased at her mood-darkening commentary.

"We've got some really solid metrics here that certainly argue against your pessimism," he countered.

Eva responded, "I believe St. Swithin's voice is being lost in the community. Several new homeless centers have opened in other areas of the city in the last three years and they seem to be at capacity. " Arnold quickly shot back, "Because they're so inexperienced, they haven't been able to solve the problem like we have."

"I don't believe that," Eva countered quickly. "Sure, we have been successful at ending homelessness for many of those we have served in the past. But we've seen a dramatic drop in people who come to our facility. Our ability to reach those who need our help has been hurt by losing our outreach person. And I see a huge change in our homeless population demographics."

Arnold, still visibly annoyed, snapped back, "Such as?"

"A huge shift—a swiftly growing Hispanic population in the past 18 months, for one," Eva responded. "We have always based our programs and outreach on the premise of our traditional homogeneous Anglo and African-American residents. We don't have anyone on staff who can speak Spanish. None of our literature, nothing on our website is going to be comprehensible to these new homeless."

Arnold reflected for a moment. "So, if we follow what you're proposing, we've got to become more visible to this changing population. You know that's going to be a real challenge, since our donations are way down."

Eva was ready for that assertion. "That's another thing. We're never going to recover from this decline without more board help in regaining our financial support. I need for you all to retrain yourselves on your marketing skills. Five years ago, the board had all sorts of energy focused on writing letters to the editor, speaking at the chamber of commerce lunches, showing how much we cared and how effective we were in resolving homelessness. Somehow, that has all gone dormant."

The rest of the board, having witnessed this exchange, began to stir. Logan, one of the few board members who recalled the era Eva was talking about, spoke up. "I'm willing to dust off and upgrade that old presentation and train any folks who might want to participate in taking it public once more. It sounds like we've got to get ourselves re-engaged if we're really going to succeed."

CHAPTER 14

LIGHTHOUSES, BUOYS, AND SEA LORE: STANDARDS AND BEST PRACTICES

Red sky in the morning, sailors take warning;
Red sky at night, sailors delight.

–Sea lore

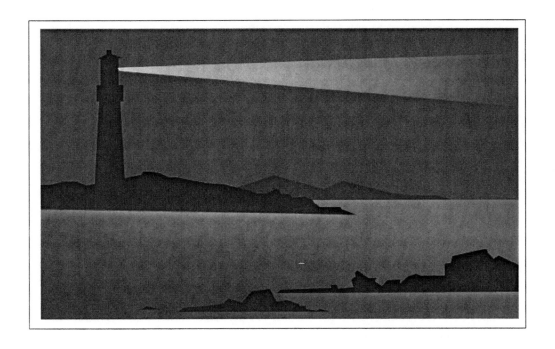

S hanice, the newly appointed board treasurer, realized that she might not be able to continue in that role, or even remain on this nonprofit board as a member, when she brought up the issue of contracting with an outside agency to conduct an external audit. The other board members all objected strongly to her suggestion.

"We have seen [the founder and executive director] Alicia build this organization literally from the ground up over the past five years," protested Greg, who served as vice chair.

"She's the most trustworthy person in the world. The last thing we need is to waste money on such an expense. An outside audit only signifies that we don't trust her!"

A number of board members nodded and murmured their support for Greg's opinion.

Shanice, who had a strong financial background in her regular job as a CPA, tried to keep her emotions in check as she rallied to make her point. "I agree that Alicia has been incredibly successful as our executive director. In a very short time, she's grown this nonprofit from almost no money to an annual budget of $550,000. I know we've been faithful as a board in our oversight of this fiscal expansion, but we're at a new stage now where our responsibility to our donors should include an approving evaluation from an external, independent financial review. The audit process will drive the credibility of our financial statements and ensure we're being faithful stewards of this fast-growing pool of donated money. I do trust Alicia. We all do. But it's foolish if we as a board allow ourselves to *blindly* trust anyone in this position. Didn't any of you read the newsletter from the state attorney general's office? External audits represent a behavior recognized as a best practice at this stage of our growth. It's a sound and conscientious act."

Shanice's persuasive comments drew a softer response from the other board members. They began to discuss the possibility of giving this matter further consideration. Later in the meeting, the board approved sending out a request for proposals from several auditing firms to find out about their process and the potential cost of providing this service.

Acknowledging and adhering to a set of standards, principles, and best practices can keep the metaphorical nonprofit ship from ripping its hull open on the treacherous, unseen rocks and shoals of inattention, indifference, and malfeasance.

Throughout mankind's seafaring history, mariners have been reliant upon various methods that warn ships about dangerous obstructions, bad weather, or other hazards that threaten a seafarer's journey. Lighthouses provide one major means of that protective signaling, giving ships a visual orienting point as well as a warning of nearby shoals and reefs. Coastlines and harbors are dotted with buoys of different sizes, shapes, and colors, all indicating information about water depth, rights of way, and other matters critical to passing ships.

In addition to these physical markers, mariners have built up a huge canon of knowledge based on the experience of hundreds of generations of sailors. This wisdom, passed on faithfully from seasoned mariners to their apprentices, covers a comprehensive array of topics—understanding the weather, the sea, the principles of sailing and navigation, as well as a rich mythology of the mysteries and wonders of an ocean-faring life.

To willfully ignore any of the physical warning signals or to pay no heed to the wisdom of sailors past greatly increases the likelihood that the nonprofit ship will not survive the many hazards that threaten a seagoing vessel.

There have been a lot of best-practice lighthouses and buoys established in the past decade to help guide nonprofit ships around those dangerous reefs and shoals. Many state-based nonprofit associations have developed specific guidelines based on the important rules and policies that need to be in place for a nonprofit to find safe passage. In addition, national organizations such as the Better Business Bureau have refreshed some of their older attempts at setting standards by creating more comprehensive programs such as the Wise Giving™ program, which is designed to give sound guidance to nonprofits about discharging their appropriate fiduciary responsibilities. Some state associations have promulgated and exported to other states a substantial list of guiding principles. A good example of this can be found in the Standards of Excellence©, which was created in Maryland and then later offered to other states as a model to be followed.

No matter which set of standards a nonprofit may want to adopt, they are all grounded in two major areas of focus. The first area has to do with sound business practices which help the organization stay financially and operationally effective and efficient. The second area focuses on developing and enhancing the organization's commitment to sound governance, transparency, and integrity.

In the pure business aspect of nonprofit operations, these standards address subjects such as managing overhead costs to ensure that most of each donated dollar goes toward mission. These guidelines also examine and recommend appropriate ratios for the amount of money the nonprofit should spend to raise money. All of these standards recommend building a robust capacity for strategic operational planning. They also outline principles concerning such things as human resource management and public advocacy.

Beyond the operational aspects, these standards speak to other critical needs, such as the organization's obligation to be transparent and accountable to its donors, to its stakeholders, and to the community as a whole. They describe strong ethical principles in the arena of fundraising and faithful compliance with donor wishes. Equally important within those standards is the detailed explanation of how boards of directors are to be formed, govern, and faithfully provide responsible oversight as guarantors to the community that the organization will, in fact, succeed.

These evolving standards of practice, especially the ones fostered by regional and national agencies, even provide a structure for compliance leading to a certification. A nonprofit meeting these rigorous standards can proudly display proof of its efficiency and integrity.

It would not be unusual if what now is displayed as exceptional might someday become a common expectation. Consider this historical maritime example. In the early nineteenth century, Great Britain's shipping industry was plagued with a great deal of lost cargo because ships were becoming overloaded. Even more tragic was the enormous loss of sailors' lives on those sinking ships. Close to a thousand sailors a year perished at sea, drowning as these overloaded ships sank beneath the waves. A man named Samuel Plimsoll campaigned to require ships to display a "load line" or mark on the exterior of the ship's hull. That marking displayed the limit of how low the ship could rest in the water once it was loaded to its maximum safe capacity. With this standard, the cargo loaders would know when a ship had reached its safe maximum capacity. This practice became quickly accepted because it saved ship lines an enormous amount of money by dramatically reducing ships and cargo lost from overloading the vessels. Ship captains and crews obviously were enthusiastic over this new standard, since it dramatically increased their safety. As a consequence of these improvements, the Plimsoll line became a worldwide standard—it's now known as the international load line—and can be found on all commercial ships.

Acknowledging and adhering to a set of standards, principles, and best practices can keep the metaphorical nonprofit ship from ripping its hull open on the treacherous, unseen rocks and shoals of inattention, indifference, and malfeasance.

No matter how much safety one might want to build into a ship, traversing the seas and oceans still conveys with it mystery, awe, and very real dangers. In order to cope with the innumerable and uncontrollable factors that a seafaring vessel must encounter, sailors have devised a long list of superstitions—beliefs and behaviors that they rely on to given them control over the many unknowns in these journeys. For example, it was once considered bad luck to begin a journey on a Friday, but good luck to begin a journey on a Sunday. Dolphins seen swimming alongside the ship were portents of a good journey, but a shark following a ship indicated that a death on board would soon follow. Women, priests, and flowers were all considered to be unlucky presences on a ship. A black cat on board, to the contrary of many land-based traditions, was said to bring good luck. Seabirds were never to be killed since they were believed to contain within them the souls of dead sailors. Cutting one's hair and fingernails while on a journey also was said to bring bad luck.

Seen from an outsider's perspective, these superstitions appear quaint and in some ways oddly fascinating. However, in a similar way, there are many people who hold similar misconceptions about nonprofits. While these are not superstitions precisely, they nonetheless represent an unhelpful and wrongheaded series of convictions that can lead to silly and—in some cases—very harmful decisions. These unquestioned "truths" lead many nonprofit ships astray. Dispelling these truths follows Mark Twain's wisdom: "It ain't what you don't know that gets you into trouble. It's what you know for sure that just ain't so."

Among the more prominent misperceptions about nonprofits are:

- Nonprofits are prohibited by law from ending their fiscal year with a "profit" or surplus. [*It's both allowed and proper for a nonprofit to build up a financial reserve that can be used in later years when it might need that extra capital.*]

- Nonprofits are prohibited from charging for their services. [*Fees have often been a legitimate form of revenue generation. Many nonprofits have always charged fees for their services. Nonprofit theaters, museums and galleries often charge fees as part of their service.*]

- Only nonprofits with staff (crew) can make any real difference. [*Vast numbers of nonprofits succeed with the help of unpaid volunteers and never reach a stage where they employ a staff.*]

- The Board of Directors can and should ignore term limits for their more important members. [*Boards benefit much more from refreshing their membership on a periodic basis rather than allowing their members to stay and become calcified.*]

- Nonprofit staff (captain and crew) are generally people who couldn't make it in the for-profit arena. [People who serve in the nonprofit arena are creative, resourceful, and highly motivated professionals whose accomplishments rival anyone in the for-profit realm.]

- People who work in the nonprofit sector (captain and crew) are all good-natured. [The nonprofit sector does not attract saints any more than the for-profit sector.]

- Wealthy board members are the best board members. [Having wealth or access to wealth can be a great characteristic; however, it is not a predictor of that director's ability to help govern.]

- The executive director (ship's captain) never needs evaluation from the board. [The captain can always benefit from the guidance, challenge, and support provided by the board's honest feedback.]

- The executive director (ship's captain) will never abandon the ship. [The captain is mortal and subject to any number of known and unknowable circumstances that could remove him or her unexpectedly.]

The best way to dispel these myths and misunderstandings is to purposely subscribe to some set of standards of practice that help guide a nonprofit in establishing operational excellence. Those standards are not just lists of empty phrases. They are proven practices that lead to mission success. They explain the rationale for their importance and clear away a lot of the misunderstandings that people often carry about governance and nonprofit performance.

Compass Points

✧ The evolving body of standards of practice for nonprofits represents a vital resource to keep the nonprofit ship from drifting into dangerous waters.

✧ A time is coming when some sort of certification from an authoritative source will become a necessary ingredient for any nonprofit to verify its integrity and competence.

✧ The body of knowledge that has formed the establishment of standards is the best source in dispelling old, dysfunctional myths about nonprofits.

Points to Consider

1. Describe how your organization might benefit from adopting standards of high performance. In what areas might your organization benefit most?

_____

_____

_____

_____

_____

_____

_____

2. What beliefs might your board hold that are contrary to the principles of high-performing nonprofits? What myths could your organization challenge and benefit from dispelling?

_____

_____

_____

_____

_____

_____

_____

It's All about the Kids

Tatyana settled into the conference room chair, ready to meet with the BB Jennings Foundation's executive committee. She was honored to have been invited to interview for a position on the board.

BB Jennings, of course, was something of a household name in this part of the state. He had achieved his early fame as a world-class racquetball champion, winning title after title in national and then international competitions. BB had literally "hung up his racquet" after spending twenty-five years in the sport and amassing a small fortune from his endorsement contracts with various racquetball equipment manufacturers.

Soon after leaving his athletic career, he became active in local politics, eventually becoming elected as the county judge. After holding that position for two terms, he established the BB Jennings Foundation to help children in poverty. The foundation has been in existence for ten years.

"Tatyana, so glad that you could join us this morning," said Llewellyn, the BB Jennings Foundation board chair.

"You know we have a very small board of directors, but we're looking to expand it to add some additional expertise. We're especially interested in your background in public relations and marketing."

Tatyana smiled at Llewellyn and the other committee members. "Well, I am certainly flattered to be considered. Can you tell me more about the foundation's mission and how it operates?"

At this point, Roger, the board's treasurer and BB Jennings' brother-in-law, took over the conversation. "Let me give you some insight into the foundation. I have been part of the board since we set up the organization ten years ago. Our mission focus is to provide money to help children out of poverty. We raise money by having Mr. Jennings autograph items such as his own brand-endorsed racquets and racquetballs at various sports conventions. He sells those at the conventions and online through our website. This generates close to $100,000 each year. We take that money and give it to the children."

Tatyana brightened at that point and asked, "That's wonderful! That kind of money must make a huge difference in helping children in our area of the state, since there's so much need in this region. Can you tell me what percent of that money actually reaches the children?"

Now Wilma, the board secretary and BB Jennings' wife, joined the conversation. "Naturally, we incur some overhead expenses, so not all the money goes to the children. My husband, Mr. Jennings, of course, is the executive director of the foundation, and since he generates the money, we pay him a salary. And then there are the overhead expenses that involve all our administration costs. Roger, you have the statistics on our expenses, don't you?"

Roger shuffled through some papers and said, "Let's see here, we pay Mr. Jennings an annual salary of $70,000. And the administrative costs associated with his travel to various sports shows and so forth amount to, let me see, approximately $10,000 per year. Then, when you add in our website administration and phones and office expense, let me see, that looks like another $12,500. So I suppose we're looking at roughly $7500 that goes to the children." Roger, Llewellyn, and Wilma all beamed warmly at that point.

Tatyana tried to hide her dismay. "I'm sure those children are very grateful," she stuttered, "and I suppose Mr. Jennings works very hard to earn all that revenue."

"Oh yes," replied Wilma, "he spends several hours every week signing that equipment."

Tatyana tried to understand more. "How does the foundation decide which children to give all that money to every year?"

"Oh, that's very easy," smiled Wilma. "We donate all that cash to our pastor at our church. Pastor Billy is Mr. Jennings' cousin. No one is more respected. The board trusts him implicitly."

Tatyana, still trying to make sense of all this, proceeded. "Can you tell me about the other board members?"

"Certainly," offered Llewellyn. "We have three other board members: They include Bob, who is also Mr. Jennings' son-in-law and who, by the way, does magnificent contract work maintaining our website. And there's Carly, Mr. Jennings' daughter, and finally, Albert, who manages Mr. Jennings' political campaigns."

Tatyana was certain that what she was hearing couldn't get any worse.

"These board members sound like they're very close to Mr. Jennings. Can you tell me why you want to offer me a position on the board? After all, I am not closely tied to Mr. Jennings through family or business connections."

Roger took up that question quickly. "We realize that we've had some adverse publicity lately, you know, people poking around asking meddling questions about our operations. So we want to show good faith to the community by diversifying our board—and it certainly would be helpful to have someone who can better help us craft our message to the community about all the good we do. Mr. Jennings is looking to take his talents to a higher state office someday, you know."

Sitting in stunned silence, facing the executive committee who all smiled benignly at her, Tatyana tried her best to be diplomatic. "I can't tell you how much it means to me to have had this chance to understand how this foundation operates. Let me think about it and I'll give you my answer tomorrow."

CHAPTER 15

CONVOYS, FLEETS, AND FLOTILLAS: JOINING WITH OTHERS

If you want to go fast, go alone.
If you want to go far, go together.

–African Proverb

Sometimes, in the metaphorical considerations of a nonprofit as a seaborne vessel, it's not a question of needing a bigger ship. It's more a matter of connecting with other ships that are traveling in the same direction.

Throughout history, ships at sea have gathered to pursue common aims. The most common examples can be found in military situations where naval ships have gathered in fleets or flotillas bound to a common destination. In Christopher Marlowe's play, *Dr. Faustus*, there's the famous reference to the mythological Helen, the "face that launched a thousand ships," referring to the Greek fleet's invasion to recapture her from Troy. Columbus had the good sense to cross the Atlantic with three ships (a wise choice, since his flagship, the *Santa Maria*, did not survive the initial return journey to Spain after the discovery of the New World). Even in the *Star Trek* series, the USS *Enterprise* is part of a larger group or "Starfleet" charged with peacekeeping, scientific, and diplomatic missions.

Consider this deeper historical example of combining sea forces. Early in World War II, Great Britain faced its most mortal danger from the sea. The strategic sea lanes connecting it to its colonies and allies were filled with supply ships delivering food to feed the British people and materials necessary to fight the war. Individual supply ships sailing alone were easy prey for the German submarines or "U-boats" that roamed the Atlantic. Those submarines sank those ships with such alarming success that Winston Churchill, Britain's prime minister during the Second World War, later wrote in his memoirs that "the only thing that ever really frightened me during the war was the U-boat peril."

The ultimate solution to this grave threat was to assemble these supply ships in formations called convoys, accompanied by armed escort ships which would fire upon the U-boats. This ultimately reversed the deadly losses, but not before the German U-boats devised a counter-strategy, attempting to attack the convoys using coordinated groups of U-boats in what the German admiralty referred to as "wolf packs."

Nonprofits come into being in a hazardous environment. They have to compete for their resources, including volunteers, board members, donors, and public awareness and goodwill. They may face substantial adversaries in the political and public-policy realm. As a consequence, many nonprofits begin their existence as fragile vessels sailing on a competitive sea. It's scarcely a wonder these vulnerable craft would be suspicious of any vessel that comes into sight. The very realization that other vessels exist, perhaps in pursuit of a similar mission, carrying similar passengers, competing for investors' support, and aimed toward an identical destination, could stir deep anxiety rather than joy.

Tragically, this sort of worldview can lead to numerous missed opportunities that could lead to mutual benefit. Seeing the other ships as enemies can block an organization's ability to defend itself against much more dangerous threats such as the vast, impersonal economic storms and political icebergs that imperil all who sail.

For any nonprofit, there are a number of benefits to be realized in connecting with other nonprofit agencies, across a whole spectrum of activities. This begins at the most fundamental level, by developing an awareness of the other organizations in the region which are pursuing similar missions to its own. The next step comes in rejecting the notion that "the other" is by definition a potential threat and moving to the presumption that they may in fact be likely allies.

Even if this form of re-thinking proves impossible for the top leadership, there is still wisdom in the age-old aphorism, originally attributed to Sun-Tzu and thousands of years later inserted into the script of *The Godfather*: "Keep your friends close and your enemies closer." The point of this counterintuitive advice maintains that staying in contact with a potential competitor puts you at greater advantage, since it allows you to stay aware of the potential adversary's interests, plans, or intentions.

To abandon the go-it-alone philosophy, a nonprofit has to employ a robust set of tactics to broaden its communication outreach to other organizations. It has to establish a reputation of authentic trust with others. It begins this process by inviting conversations with the other nonprofit ships it encounters. These conversations can be as simple and direct as asking to hold an introductory session between the captains (executive directors) to exchange basic information about organizational missions. The point of these conversations centers on finding areas of joint interest and potential mutual benefit. Even if no mutual areas of jointly held advantage emerge from these talks, the very act of outreach and contact sets the stage for further conversation, if conditions warrant.

These initial interactions can lead to a series of deeper mutual benefits in the form of cooperation, coordination, and collaboration.

Cooperation means working together for a common purpose and shared benefit. For example, if two organizations have a joint need to find expanded or enhanced physical space to house their growing operations, they may agree to cooperate with one another to find a common office space, one that would accommodate both of their needs and perhaps even offer discounted rental costs to each, since two agencies would bring a greater combined demand for space and services.

Let's assume that these two organizations work together to research possible sites and through their mutual efforts compare and contrast their findings, negotiate with one another to determine the most advantageous shared site, and then decide to approach their chosen landlord.

At this point, they are ready to move to the second stage of interaction: coordination. Coordination involves entities engaged in the harmonious interaction of timing and sequencing events. In this case, they may coordinate their interactions and negotiation talks with the property owners. If they negotiate a successful contract, the agencies may later coordinate their efforts in moving into the space, ensuring that they don't interrupt one another's progress.

> For any nonprofit, there are a number of benefits to be realized in connecting with other nonprofit agencies, across a whole spectrum of activities.

At a later point, these two jointly-located organizations may move to an even more advanced stage of interaction: collaboration. Collaboration represents one of the highest stages of mutual interaction, aimed at a deep commitment to combining skills at all levels to solve problems or find creative new approaches to operational challenges. This stage involves a more complex practice, involving more people at different levels of each organization communicating, defining roles, and working closely in the search for, and implementation of, new solutions to common needs.

For example, several collaborating organizations may agree that they each want to rid themselves of the cost of operating a fleet of vehicles to transport the people they serve to their program sites. These collaborating agencies may have, through their combined needs, enough people who need transport that it may make much more sense to contract with a local transport carrier—perhaps the local city bus service—to provide specialized, defined, conveyance services. In this instance, one agency may not have enough demand to make this an economically feasible alternative, but the combined demand of both agencies would provide the right volume, reaching an economy of scale to make this a workable, cost-saving alternative for both nonprofits.

Beyond the significant Big 3 "C's" of cooperation, coordination, and collaboration lies the last, ultimate stage of interaction: that of organizational mergers. Of course, cooperation, coordination, and collaboration do not inevitably lead to this final stage of interconnected relations between nonprofits. Even so, it does merit some consideration as the final, although not inevitable, stage of connecting with others.

Mergers should be an option when the operational and financial conditions of those agencies involved point to dramatic potential for significant combined mission success. Mergers represent the most complex and difficult stage of nonprofit interconnectivity and, as such, take considerable amounts of analysis, negotiation, time, and trust. When accomplished properly, mergers yield more comprehensive benefits to stakeholders, donors, and the community. They traditionally bring about significant efficiencies, dramatically cutting overhead costs, allowing

212

more donated resources to flow directly into program services that advance mission success.

A merger can be an option when, sadly, a nonprofit ship can go further. It may have exhausted its resources, suffered too much wear and tear, or so lost its way that its board of directors (owners) will decide that it is no longer seaworthy. At that stage, the owners are duty-bound to signal for some other vessel to come and pick up its remaining passengers.

Mergers produce great positive change but also stir significant anxiety. When the two ships decide they can combine into one larger, more efficient ship, the inevitable issue arises: under the command of one ship, they don't need two captains, two crews, or, for that matter, two sets of directors (owners). Resolving this question represents one of the toughest challenges of the merger. Under whose command will the new vessel sail? With which set—or blend—of crew? And finally, the decision must be made: Which set—or combination—of owners will be responsible for the oversight of this new vessel? Beyond those issues are even more vexing logistics such as re-tooling programs, addressing issues of the physical plant, administration, technology, relationships with other agencies, donors, and most important, those being served by the mission.

Compass Points

⬦ The concept of going it alone in today's nonprofit world is strategically unsustainable.

⬦ Some form of outreach to other nonprofits should always be practiced.

⬦ Nonprofits can benefit from knowing and using the basic tools of such outreach: communication, cooperation, coordination, and collaboration.

⬦ Mergers, though complex and rare, should always be a consideration if circumstances for mission success are compelling.

Points to Consider

1. How would you describe your current community of nonprofits? Do you have a concept of how many there are, how diverse they are in mission, and their relative budget sizes?

_____

_____

_____

_____

_____

_____

_____

2. How would you describe your "ship's" practice of initiating or responding to offers to communicate with other nonprofits in your sea lanes?

_____

_____

_____

_____

_____

_____

_____

3. What opportunities exist in your community to foster intercommunication among the nonprofits that may lead to greater trust and understanding? What could your organization do to sponsor such a process?

_____

_____

_____

_____

_____

_____

_____

4. Describe a historic instance where your vessel has engaged in coordination, cooperation, or collaboration. In what ways did that activity help or harm your mission effectiveness?

_____

_____

_____

_____

_____

_____

_____

5. Has anyone in your region witnessed the merger of any nonprofits in recent history? What were the mission results? What lessons did the community learn?

_____

_____

_____

_____

_____

_____

_____

Unlikely Allies

In a small Midwestern community, a group of twenty small nonprofits assembled on a wintry Saturday morning. Summoned by two regional foundations, the purpose of the session was to explore more efficient ways of using foundation grant dollars.

Regina, the executive director of Foundation A, explained to the assembled executive staff from these nonprofits that the available funding projections for the next several years were going to be sharply diminished due to the shrinking pool of the foundation's investments.

"I'm here to be as clear as I can," Regina continued. "We're going to insist on funding only those organizations that look to use our money to address mission problems in ways that engage the wider community. That means that in every grant application, we're going to be looking very specifically for ways in which you will work with one another."

As if the winter temperatures weren't chilling enough, the room atmosphere turned even colder at this news. The regional nonprofits had a longstanding tradition of fierce competition for Foundation A's money. That history had created a well-understood proverb in this community: every dollar your agency receives means one dollar less for my agency—a clear example of win/lose in every application.

"We've come to realize that our past practices have only encouraged competition among you, and that's had an isolating effect on your efforts," Regina explained. "Everyone has become insulated from one another, focusing only on their one specific aspect of need. This narrowness leaves gaps in community coverage, and that only gives rise to more nonprofits forming, adding more demand for our diminishing funds. This has got to be reversed. So, here's the message: we'll be very open to those applications that show a strong inclination to work in common with other agencies to advance mission success."

During the brief intermission, before Stan from Foundation B was about to present a similar demand, the executive directors milled about the coffee urns, muttering their disbelief.

"It'll be a much colder day than this in Hell before I link my organization with any of these others," Aubrey sputtered to a fellow executive director. Aubrey's nonprofit, a local historic foundation, was one of the more well-off groups present, insulated from the economic downturns since 2008 by relying on a very generous (though significantly reduced) endowment. But the very fact that she was expressing an opinion to Roger, the executive director of an animal rescue group, and a man to whom she would otherwise never have given the time of day, was a surprise to all who witnessed the interaction.

Roger was a bit more sanguine. "I don't object to the concept of working with others," he replied. "I just haven't had any experience at it, or any reason to—at least until today." Aubrey moved away, heading back to her seat, shaking her head in wonder.

Others in the huddled group murmured noncommittally. Since this group rarely assembled in one space, they weren't comfortable in one another's presence and were reluctant to say much other than to commiserate over this new challenge.

After the break, Stan presented his views. "We realize that working together is a lost art in this region, so we're going to sponsor a series of sessions—for free—to all the nonprofits, where we will bring in speakers from other cities that have fostered nonprofit cooperation. We think their lessons can give us all ideas and encouragement."

Aubrey snorted under her breath to her chief financial officer, "Just what I need—a series of classes from so-called experts! As if I don't have enough on my plate."

The executive director of the local food bank, Neville, overhearing Aubrey, whispered to her, "Come on, Aubrey, you're the one who's always promoting community learning at your historic homes. Now is your chance." Aubrey just glared at him.

Stan continued to outline the planned series. "We'll schedule six of these sessions. Aside from the testimonials, we'll bring in experts who can help us all understand the steps in cooperation, coordination, and collaboration. They'll even facilitate discussions on how we may find common interaction."

Later in the session, after answering questions, Stan and Regina passed along the sign-up sheets and were encouraged when fifteen of the attendees indicated that they were willing to attend.

Over the next six weeks, the attendees faithfully showed up every Tuesday morning for three hours to listen and learn from the Foundations' guest speakers. Aside from deepening their understanding of the advantages of organizational interaction, they simply got to know one another and their respective challenges better through these shared experiences. As they participated in the last two meetings, where they tried to find mutual opportunities for common benefit, the struggles began.

The level of trust and communication that had risen as a consequence of the early meetings had helped reduce the suspicions that plagued this community, but there were few who felt ready to risk significant interaction. Two agencies, neither of whom had anything close to a shared mission, eventually came to realize that they could benefit from sharing physical space—one of them had just entered into a lease and had extra space which was just the right size for another agency's new satellite office. They were delighted with this surprising mutual discovery. The only other agreement that came from this session was that five participants agreed to set up a volunteer database that they would share with one another and eventually with others who might want to join.

A week later, Stan and Regina reviewed the results of their six-week session. "Not a great deal of improvement," remarked Stan. "We're only seeing seven organizations out of the original twenty taking any steps. And those may not come to any real success."

Regina thought for a few moments. "I think we should be happy with the few we're able to influence. We should do all we can to support their fledgling efforts. You know, somehow celebrate any success they may have, especially in these embryonic stages. These behaviors take a while to take root and flourish. Their eventual success will attract others, especially when it becomes clear that they are saving money and building their mission effectiveness."

CHAPTER 16

HOMEWARD BOUND

'We shall not cease from exploration
And the end of all our exploring
Will be to arrive where we started
And know the place for the first time.

– T.S. Eliot

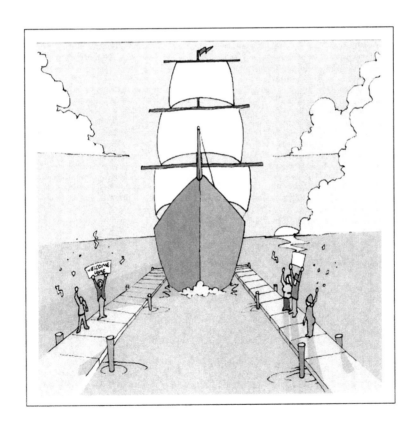

The ninety-year-old farmer's life was drawing to a close. He had summoned his children around him as he lay on his deathbed. In the course of murmuring his last wishes about the farm, which had been in the family for over two hundred years, he turned toward his eldest son and whispered, "You can sell off the land and all the farm equipment after I'm gone. But whatever you do, don't ever part with that antique ax that hangs in the barn near the front door. It once belonged to George Washington."

All of the old man's children stared at one another and then back at their father in astonishment. "Dad," whispered the eldest son, "you never told us that before. Are you sure it belonged to Washington? It never seemed that old to us when we used it in our chores."

Oh, yes," the dying farmer assured him, "It was his for sure. Now, the handle has been replaced three times, and that blade has been changed five times, I think. But it was definitely George Washington's ax."

In Portsmouth, England, visitors can visit the HMS *Victory*, the ship Lord Nelson commanded in the defeat of Napoleon's French fleet at the Battle of Trafalgar in 1805. The ship sits in dry dock in Portsmouth, the oldest commissioned ship in the world (30 years older than the USS *Constitution*). It has survived numerous brushes with extinction. Various naval officials considered scrapping it over the past two centuries. It even took bomb damage during the German blitz bombings in World War II. Over its 250-year history, the *Victory* has undergone numerous restorations. Of the 3,500 tons of lumber that make up this ship, only the English elm keel is part of the original ship.

In both of these examples, the essence of each object somehow remains, despite the overwhelming physical changes they have undergone.

Nonprofit organizations contain a similar transcendent essence. Despite everything else, the vision endures, prompting owners, captain, and crew to stay true to the promise to all passengers. The ship may evolve and grow over time, from a small rowboat to a mighty tall ship. It will carry many passengers, fulfilling its promise to deliver those traveling on it to a promised, better future. The founder, successive owners, captain, crews will represent different eras of the ship's lifetime, but the enduring aspect of that nonprofit ship will be this: a transcendent promise to serve the passengers and so fulfill its promise to build a better world.

> Despite everything else, the vision endures, prompting owners, captain, and crew to stay true to the promise to all passengers.

225

Bibliography

Berman, Michael, and David Brown. *The Power of Metaphor: Story Telling & Guided Journeys for Teachers, Trainers & Therapists.* Carmarthen: Crown House Publishing, Ltd., 2000.

Geary, James. *I Is an Other: The Secret Life of Metaphor and How It Shapes the Way We See the World.* New York: HarperCollins, 2008.

Mersey, Viscount John Charles Bigham (1st baron.), and Hon. Arthur i.e. Somerset Arthur Gough-Calthorpe. *Loss of the Steamship "Titanic": Report of a Formal Investigation Into the Circumstances Attending the Foundering on April 15, 1912, of the British Steamship "Titanic", of Liverpool, After Striking Ice in Or Near Latitude 41°46' N., Longitude 50°14' W., North Atlantic Ocean.* Washington, DC: U.S. Government Printing Office, 1912.

Morgan, Gareth. *Images of Organization.* Thousand Oaks, CA: Sage Publications, Inc., 2006.

Sinek, Simon. *Start with Why: How Great Leaders Inspire Everyone to Take Action.* New York: Portfolio, 2009.

Kentucky School of Art

MISSION:

The Kentucky School of Art opens the door to a creative and productve life through a higher education in the visual arts.

VISION:

The vision for KSA is to become a college with art at its center: All disciplines and studies will branch out from this core. Through the lens of art, students will study in the necessary courses to guide their individualized exploration, development, and the expression of their creative spirit. In addition, KSA will engage nationally recognized faculty and artists to nurture students' creative practice though exposure to traditional and contemporary art practices.

LOCATION:

A new venture in the secure environment of Spalding University's urban campus, the Kentucky School of Art is located in the South Broadway neighborhood of Louisville, Kentucky, at 845 South 3rd Street near downtown.

INTERN CHRIS AUSTERMAN:

Chris Austerman is a rising star at The Kentucky School of Art at Spalding University. In designing and illustrating *Shipshape*, he fulfilled his internship with Old Stone Press and has shown he is a promising illustrator and fine artist. Chris recently received a scholarship from the Italian Cultural Institute of Louisville to enroll in the International School of Drawing, Painting, and Sculpture in Umbria, Italy, as part of the KSA Study Abroad program.

About The Center for Nonprofit Excellence (CNPE)

CNPE is dedicated to co-creating a vibrant, exemplary nonprofit community in Greater Louisville through collaboration, shared learning, advocacy, and the promotion of innovation and excellence.

Founded in 1999, the Center for Nonprofit Excellence is a 501(c)(3) nonprofit management service organization that provides a central point to access information about the nonprofit sector, promulgates best practices, instructs in the realm of board and staff professional enrichment, and offers individualized consultation, all to advance the sector's quest to serve in and around the region of Louisville, Kentucky.

Serving over 360 regional nonprofit members who subscribe to its services, CNPE also enjoys the membership support of 15 area foundations, 42 individuals, and 38 corporate sponsors.

CNPE's office is located in downtown Louisville in the ArtSpace building.

Center for Nonprofit Excellence
323 West Broadway, Suite 501, Louisville, Kentucky 40202
502.315.2673 I www.cnpe.org

About the Author

Eric Schmall has been in consulting and management for over forty years. For most of that era, he worked in the private sector in various capacities as a research analyst, manager, and consultant.

In 2001, Eric joined Louisville's Center for Nonprofit Excellence (CNPE) as Director of Consultation. In 2006, Eric earned his designation as a licensed consultant with the Standards for Excellence® Institute, a national initiative that promotes the highest standards of ethics and accountability in the social sector.

Since joining CNPE, Eric has successfully designed and facilitated over a thousand meetings, retreats, workshops, and seminars on leadership, board governance, project management, systems theory, board development, and strategic planning cycles for hundreds of nonprofit organizations in the Kentucky and Southern Indiana region. In 2010, he authored his first book, *Striving for Excellence in the Social Sector,* which chronicled a decade's worth of exemplary achievements in the nonprofit sector in the Louisville, Kentucky and Southern Indiana region.

He is a native of Louisville, Kentucky and has spent most of his career in that community.

Eric can be reached at CNPE via his direct phone number: 502.618. 5329 or by email: eschmall@cnpe.org

CPSIA information can be obtained at www.ICGtesting.com
Printed in the USA
LVOW110742090713

341807LV00002B/4/P

9 781938 462061